The Harpenden to Hemel Hempstead Railway

The Nickey Line

by
Sue & Geoff Woodward

THE OAKWOOD PRESS

© Oakwood Press & Sue & Geoff Woodward 1996

British Library Cataloguing in Publication Data
A Record for this book is available from the British Library
ISBN 0 85361 502 0

Typeset by Oakwood Graphics.
Repro by Ford Graphics, Ringwood, Hants.
Printed by Alpha Print (Oxford) Ltd, Witney, Oxon.

Ex-MR compound 4-4-0 No. 1029 passes through Harpenden station, 19th October, 1929.
H.C. Casserley

Published by
The Oakwood Press
P.O. Box 122, Headington, Oxford OX3 8LU

Contents

Redbourn station *c.* 1920.   *Authors' Collection*

A picture postcard view of Hemel Hempstead. *Authors' Collection*

A turn of the century view of Harpenden Lane, Redbourn. *Authors' Collection*

Introduction

The 1801 Census revealed a population of 3,680 in Hemel Hempstead. The town was small, reasonably compact but lacked industrial development. Instead it concentrated on agriculture and held a thriving market. By 1851 the population had almost doubled, with industries becoming established. John Dickinson owned an expanding paper-making business at Apsley Mills and a vast cottage industry was engaged in straw plait production, using reeds from the nearby Gade Valley.

During the second quarter of the century proposals to bring a railway line to Hemel Hempstead as part of the London to Birmingham route were thwarted by landowners who did not want to see the local Moor disfigured. This Moor, known as Boxmoor, comprised a large area of common land situated between Hemel Hempstead and the hamlet of Boxmoor, and was supervised by an influential body, the Boxmoor Trust. The promoters of the London & Birmingham scheme were therefore forced to construct their railway on the side of the Moor furthest from the town, and it opened between London and its temporary terminus at Boxmoor on 20th July, 1837. Thus, the old town of Hemel Hempstead was left without rail or canal connection, since the Grand Junction Canal had also been built on the furthest side of the Moor.

However, as time passed, the tide of local opinion in favour of providing better transport facilities became more pronounced, perhaps because industrialists were beginning to hold influential positions in the ever-expanding town, and in the spring of 1862, as a result of one man's efforts, a firm proposal was put forward to link Hemel Hempstead town by rail to the main line at Boxmoor.

This man was John William Grover, C.E., born in 1836 at Burnham, Bucks., the son of a clergyman. Following education at Marlborough College and in Germany, he worked for Sir John Fowler, carrying out surveys for railways in Spain and Portugal. He then became a draughtsman, and later Head of Engineering at the Science & Art Department, working on South Kensington Museum and the Royal Horticultural Society's conservatory. In January 1862, at the age of 25, he set up his own engineering consultancy at Westminster.

Having family connections with Hemel Hempstead through his uncle, a solicitor who lived in the town, and being aware of a local desire for improved communications, it would appear he saw an opportunity to create a small railway which could be constructed quickly and easily, and be an asset to the community. He could also make a name for himself at the start of his own business venture. He therefore surveyed, drafted plans, estimated building costs and called a meeting to test public opinion.

The *Herts Guardian*, on 15th March, 1862, announced details of the project and added 'it is surprising that it should have been so long unattempted'. It also informed its readers that the scheme was 'likely to be supported by some influential persons in London, who are only waiting to test the feeling of the neighbourhood before coming forward', and in a later edition told of 'an eminent London capitalist who has come forward to relieve the townspeople of the costs', but no name was given.

However, on 22nd March, the newspaper broke the news that another 'more comprehensive' scheme was afoot. This new scheme was much grander - for a railway extending from Grover's proposed line and heading several miles east to join the Great Northern line at Harpenden. It was reckoned that a capital of £70,000 would be needed but a warning was given that 'practical engineers say it will never be completed for that sum'. What it did not tell its readers was that the man at the forefront of this opposing plan was none other than Mr Samuel Stallon, chief clerk in the solicitor's office of Grover's uncle!

So the scene was set, and the story which unfolded through the ensuing 15 years became a fascinating mixture of determination and disappointment, legal battles and long-winded negotiations, Acts passed and Bills rejected, financial hardship . . . and eventual success.

Our Local Express.   *C. Hewitt*

Chapter One

The First Act

The public meeting was duly held at the Town Hall on 27th March, 1862 with Mr Austin, the Bailiff, presiding. Mr Grover addressed the meeting at length on the advantages of his plan, which showed a line commencing in the coal yard at Boxmoor station, from where it crossed the Moor and the canal, and continued almost alongside the River Gade as far as Bury Mill - a distance of about 1¾ miles. He considered this route was 'made for a railway' because of the mainly flat land and lack of severance of property (something land-owners strongly disliked, and which increased the amount of compensation payable by a developing railway company). About midway between Boxmoor station and the town a line, a few hundred yards long, was shown running off to connect with Boxmoor Wharf on the Grand Junction Canal.

The estimated cost was given as £15,273 for building and £3,660 for rolling stock. £2,500 had to be included for stations, but by erecting temporary buildings £1,200 could be deducted. Grover announced a share capital of £20,000 which allowed enough to cover the cost of obtaining an Act, plus general legal expenses. He said he had given consideration to an alternative route, with a station behind Marlowes on the St Albans Road, but this was discounted on the grounds that it would cost half as much again.

In an endeavour to convert his audience, he listed the following:

1. An impetus to trade
2. Saving of time to persons travelling
3. Reduction in cost of conveying goods and passengers
4. Saving of wear and tear on roads
5. Communication with the canal wharf for coal
6. Increase in value of adjoining property
7. An encouragement to persons seeking their abode outside London to choose Hemel Hempstead
8. Boxmoor would be raised to become 1st class in rank
9. Passenger tickets would be 6*d.*, 4*d.* and 2*d.*

In addition to passenger services Grover envisaged a great deal of goods traffic, including corn, cattle, coal, flour, farm produce, manure, timber and straw. He was of the opinion that the line could be completed in a year and, somewhat triumphantly, added that it did not interfere with any other line and could not be opposed since it merely aimed at local improvement. Feeling very bold, he even declared that 'a start could be made next week if the landowners agreed. There would be no need to wait for the Act - the Contractors would take responsibility for that!'

At this point Mr Stallon called upon Mr Stocken to explain the alternative route - namely a line from Boxmoor with stations at Hemel Hempstead, Cupid Green and Redbourn, finally linking with the Great Northern Company's station at Harpenden (East). Surveyors' reports were promised for three weeks' time and a Mr Clements proposed that, in order to have all the facts before deciding which line should gain support, the meeting should adjourn for three weeks. Mr Stocken, obviously sensing some support, promised the report in two weeks and a two-week adjournment was voted through.

At the reconvened meeting on 10th April, held at the Corn Exchange, Mr Austin was again in the chair. Stallon's followers had enlisted the support of former Great Northern Engineer, Mr Brydone, who had surveyed their proposed line and estimated a cost of £9,000 per mile. He suggested that there were no difficult gradients or tunnels, and only one engine would be needed.

John Grover immediately objected. He disliked the station at Hemel Hempstead being sited on a curve, was convinced the London & North Western Railway Company (LNWR) (formerly London & Birmingham Railway Company) would oppose the scheme, and suggested that if a longer line were to be built it should link with St Albans and the Hatfield branch, thus connecting Hitchin, Watford, St Albans and Hertford.

In defence of his own plan, Grover told the meeting that 'the gentleman in London would only support the short line, provided it was the unanimous conclusion of the meeting'. This did not deter the other camp and a great deal of discussion followed, during which it was said that the second plan would not have come about at all, but for the sake of opposing the first!

Eventually a proposal was put forward for the meeting to adopt the line to Harpenden, but before a vote could be taken one gentleman observed that he would rather support a line which would cost the townspeople nothing, and an amendment was put to adopt Grover's plan. At this point the meeting became so disorganised and confused that the vote, when taken, was so uncertain that two versions of the result reached the local newspaper, as follows:

1. The Chairman then proceeded to put the resolution and an attempt was made to count the hands, but because of the confusion this proved impossible. It seemed, however, that the meeting was in favour of the original Hemel Hempstead line. *and*

2. The Chairman put the amendment to the meeting but declared he could not count the hands held up in favour of it. The original proposition was then put and it was evident there was a majority in favour of it - the numbers being said to be 50 for the amendment and 90 for the proposition, giving a majority of 40 for the Harpenden line.

It would appear that in the attendant chaos no-one knew exactly which line they were voting for, and to add to the confusion, the hands of some boys who were not entitled to vote had also been raised. The Chairman had tried to separate the voters to opposite sides of the room, but this had proved impossible. Even so, a vote of thanks was delivered to the Chairman before the meeting disbanded.

Without a mandate for either line, both sides retired to lick their wounds - both ultimately deciding to go forward with their plans. Mr Stallon's supporters published a Prospectus for their line, under the title 'The West Herts Junction Railway', but it would appear their ideas were short-lived, as no trace exists of it in either Great Northern or Parliamentary records. However, a land development plan for Hemel Hempstead does exist with this line of railway marked and named on it.

John Grover, on the other hand, pressed on more purposefully, and with his supporters established the 'Hemel Hempsted & London & North Western Railway Company' - a title which could be taken to imply the support of the latter company. (Note: the company used the alternative spelling of 'Hempsted' in its title, but for continuity we shall use the present 'Hempstead' throughout this history.) Grover prepared a final plan and drafted a Bill, dated 10th November, 1862, which was handed in at the St Albans office of the Clerk of the Peace for Hertfordshire, at 1.30 pm on 28th November. The plan showed 'a line commencing by a junction with the LNWR at a point immediately adjoining the east end of the up line platform at Boxmoor Station and terminating at or near Bury Mill End, immediately to the west bank of the overflow from the River Gade, where the river flows under the road'.

Early in January 1863 the Hemel company had written to the Board of the Grand Junction Canal seeking permission to cross the canal, and by February the Standing Orders of the House of Commons relative to the application for their line had been applied for. In late February the canal company lodged an official objection to the line, obviously fearing a loss of trade.

At about the same time a meeting of the Board of Surveyors of Highways of Hemel Hempstead was convened to discuss a letter from the Board of Trade relating to a plan by Grover's company to alter road levels under the new line. It would appear that, already, Grover was trying to reduce costs, since lowering road levels would reduce the height of bridges and embankments, but this alerted local minds to the possibility of flooding. Grover also offered to shorten the line if the Board of Trade would not allow a level crossing over Alma Street (this would have reduced the line by almost half). It is not surprising that Grover's proposals received a cool reception - Mr Stallon and two of his West Herts colleagues were members of the Highways Board! Despite a unanimous vote to keep levels of roads as they were, the Hemel company continued to be optimistic, and that optimism was rewarded when Grover's Bill became an Act, passing through Parliament on 13th July, 1863.

The first Directors were named as John Barrow (believed to be the 'eminent London capitalist'), Henry Balderson (a local businessman and member of the Boxmoor Trust), James Stuart Tulk, John Rennie Fulton and Charles Lempriere. The first paragraph of the Act states 'the persons named with others are willing at their own expense to carry such undertaking into execution'. John Barrow was a man of diverse dealings, being Chairman of the Staveley Coal & Iron Company, Chairman of the Manchester & Milford Railway Company and also a merchant in partnership with his brother, Richard, trading mainly with Spain. He was a wealthy landowner, who was already in his 70s when his association with the Hemel company began.

The Act authorised a capital of £20,000 (in £10 shares) together with a loan of £6,600 which could be taken up when half the share capital had been paid up.

With regard to the connection at Boxmoor, the Act specified that it should be 'by means of a siding at such place as the L.N.W. agree to, and not otherwise'. In actual fact, the proposed connection would have played havoc with the

LNWR goods yard and sidings, so it was perhaps forseeable that the latter would not welcome the Hemel company's ideas, despite the attraction of increased revenue.

It must be remembered that although it had registered 'London & North Western' into its title, the Hemel company could not automatically claim their support and co-operation, and the Act carried a clause making provision for settlement of disagreements through arbitration. However, the Act anticipated that the LNWR would ultimately work the line, and made provision for that company to supply hardware and staff to protect the junction, but first any agreement between the two companies must receive the assent of three-fifths of the voters of each company before the Board of Trade would accept it.

Powers of compulsory purchase were allowed for two years, with work to be completed in four, and many clauses to protect the canal company were also included. A sum of £1,721 had been paid by the Hemel company, being £1,600 (8 per cent of the total cost of the line plus interest) as a Bond until the line was completed, or half the capital expended on the work in the time allowed.

Exactly one month after obtaining its Act, the Hemel company served notice of compulsory purchase on the Boxmoor Trustees for acquisition of a part of the Moor. In an effort to humour the Trustees, the company agreed to provide cattle arches in the railway embankment. The Moor was used for grazing and these arches would allow animals to be herded from one pasture to another without danger to them or the railway.

The company also commenced negotiations with the LNWR to secure its junction, but after two years of hard bargaining no agreements had been reached. In fact, the LNWR ultimately declined to assist in any way, requesting such terms for making the required alterations at Boxmoor that it became hopeless for the smaller company to expect any support at all.

Rough Down from the moor, Boxmoor, with the Grand Union Canal in the foreground.
Authors' Collection

Chapter Two

The Second Act

Because of the company's failure to agree terms for a connection at Boxmoor there was little point starting on the physical construction of the railway, and so, after much delay and disappointment, they were forced to look elsewhere. It was an obvious choice to return to the idea of Stallon's line, an idea now strengthened by the fact that the Midland Railway Company (MR) was pressing on with its London Extension Line (Bedford to St Pancras), giving a wider choice of companies to court within a short distance of each other at Harpenden. John Barrow remained loyal and supported an extended scheme, but John Grover's name is missing from the plan which emerged. Instead Mr G.W. Hemans was Consulting Engineer and Mr A. Ormsby, the Engineer. Perhaps Grover favoured continuing with his short line; after all, he had public support and £19,530 of the £20,000 share capital had been raised. At the time the new plans were being prepared Grover was also preoccupied with his own affairs, as in March 1864 he married and in April 1865 his first son was born.

However, the new extension plan was deposited with the Clerk of the Peace at 5.40 pm on 30th November, 1864. It showed a line leaving the authorised line of 1863 and followed approximately the route as later built through Hemel Hempstead, but with a 1,200 yds-long tunnel through Highfield. Having passed Wood End Farm, and through Redbourn, it would have come round to the south end of Harpenden, via Hatchen (Hatching) Green and across Harpenden Common to join the Midland Main Line just north of the famous Skew Bridge over Southdown Road.

A second plan was included showing the line continuing from Harpenden Common, over the top of the Midland line by means of a bridge situated adjacent to Skew Bridge, then tunnelling 660 yards through the ridge before joining the Hertford, Luton & Dunstable branch of the Great Northern Railway just north of its Harpenden station. Although smooth gradients were planned, the tunnels would have proved very costly, and the proposal received considerable opposition from Harpenden landowners. It is not surprising that Parliament, in its 1865 Session, refused the idea.

Whatever impression is gained of the Hemel Hempstead company as the story unravels, one must admire its unwillingness to accept defeat. By June 1865 the time allowed by its 1863 Act for compulsory purchase had almost expired, and no other railway company had agreed to work with it, but on the 12th June the company served a further notice on the Boxmoor Trustees to purchase land, this time to include a herdsman's cottage and garden.

To complicate matters, although compulsory purchase notices were sent out in 1863, by October 1865 no agreement had been reached between the company and the Trust as to the value of the required land. On 20th October, 1865 John Barrow and George English Spencer of the Hemel company were named in a Bond for £686 19s., which sum had been paid into the Bank of England, to be paid to the Trust in respect of the land. This implies that the railway company had taken it upon itself to value the land and pay for it without reference to the Trust. Thinking this was in order, it had even gone as far as taking possession of the land, and on 27th October began some groundwork. Of course, the Trust could hardly be expected to accept this situation, and on 13th November its solicitor, Mr Day, served on Mr Butler, Secretary of the Hemel company, a notice to pay compensation at the rate of £400 per acre, and giving the company 21 days to issue a notice of appeal to the Sheriff of Hertford if it disagreed with the amount and wished to summon a jury to decide the issue.

On 23rd November the company served such notice, stating £250 per acre, but on the same day arranged a meeting between it and the Trust at which Mr Barlow (surveyor and land agent appointed by the company to negotiate land purchase) produced a ground plan of the railway showing the need to acquire yet another section of the Moor, near Cotterells Road. The question of compensation was discussed and the Chairman of the Trustees told Barlow that if the company would increase to £300 per acre, plus legal and surveyors' fees, he could probably persuade the Trustees to accept. One Trustee pressed for £350 but no seconder was found. Mr Barlow agreed to urge his Directors to increase their offer and promised to communicate their answer in a few days. In fact, it was the next day that the figure of £300 per acre was confirmed in writing, and shortly afterwards the company took possession of the land near Cotterells Road - but still no money was paid over.

At this stage one must admire the company's nerve, for it had allowed work to start on a railway across Trust land, which had been taken but not fully paid for, without a hope of realising a connection with the LNWR at Boxmoor and with an alternative route east recently rejected by Parliament. Undaunted, it prepared yet another plan, with a 'converted' Grover back as Engineer - again pushing east to Harpenden, but by another route. This plan was deposited with the Clerk of the Peace at 5.54 pm on 30th November, 1865, and received its Royal Assent on 16th July, 1866.

The new route extended from the authorised line through Hemel Hempstead and Redbourn, and then took a northerly curve around Harpenden, crossing the turnpike road (A1081), then passing under the Midland line before joining the Great Northern line at Harpenden (East). It is apparent that there was some cordiality between the Hemel company and the Great Northern (GNR), because after the plan had been submitted to Parliament the GNR decided that, as the proposed junction would interfere with its own workings, a new plan needed to be drawn up.

This was done and signed by the GNR's Mr Seymour Clarke and Messrs Grover and Henry Moon for the Hemel company. It is worth mentioning here that the GNR and LNWR were at this time jointly operating at Dunstable, and maybe the Hemel company was hoping a similar arrangement could be agreed to persuade the LNWR to allow connection at Boxmoor.

However, in an effort to come to terms with somebody, the plan also provided for a spur on to the Midland Railway's new London Extension, just north of Harpenden, and a Clause in the Act stated that where both companies required the use of the same land 'the Midland Railway Company may and shall sell . . . an Easement or Right of using the same for the purposes of enabling the (Hemel) Company to construct and maintain the railways and works herein described'.

Compulsory purchase powers were granted for three years under the new Act, with the line to be completed in four. It allowed a capital of £170,000 with power to borrow on mortgage a further £56,000. The estimated cost was put at £161,282 and Barrow paid the 8 per cent deposit. Running powers were left open for any of the companies, but a 4-furlong section of line authorised under the 1863 Act between Cotterells and Bury Mill End was formally abandoned - Grover's initial scheme was dead!

Meanwhile, the Boxmoor Trust was still endeavouring to obtain some more money from the Hemel company, without success. On 16th February, 1866 Mr Day had sent an Abstract of Title to the company which had been retained, but no payment made, and even after both parties' Solicitors had agreed measurements of land taken, still no funds were forthcoming. On the basis of £300 per acre the amount of compensation due totalled £2,100 18s. 9d.

Following receipt of the 1866 Act the company seemed to be on a new wave of enthusiasm and ambition. Instead of immediately getting down to the business of constructing its railway the company prepared another plan - this time to extend in the opposite direction to Chesham. The route would have been by way of a line leaving the Moor near where the line from Harpenden was to run in, across the LNWR main line by a bridge of 47 ft span and 14 ft high, then following the contour to Chesham. A siding was proposed to link the LNWR to the system on the opposite side of the new bridge. A short spur up to Roughdown Road Bridge (Hemel Hempstead) was also mentioned (this was part of Grover's original line, with a connection to LNWR metals via the goods yard).

The line was promoted as an aid to trade between the towns of Chesham, Hemel Hempstead, Harpenden and Luton, with particular regard to the straw plait industry, but more importantly it would have provided a bigger carrot to dangle in front of the LNWR in respect of connection at Boxmoor. In order not to show allegiance to any particular railway company the Hemel company also proposed as part of the Bill to change its name to 'The Bucks & Herts Union Railway Company'. The plan was deposited with the Clerk of the Peace at 5.30 pm on 30th November, 1866, with John Grover again acting as Engineer. However, it failed to gain Parliamentary approval, and the company was stuck with its original name!

According to a plan submitted at that time, the Hemel company's original line was constructed as far as the canal bridge in one direction and the (now A41) road in the other direction - a distance of only a few yards. Part of the planned route between the road and the LNWR station was marked as arable land, but owned by the company. A further section by Cotterells Road was marked 'under construction'.

Failure to commence construction of the Harpenden extension could be explained by suggesting that the company was awaiting the outcome of the Chesham Bill, but much more likely it was due to its inability to raise the required finance. Money would have been leaving the company's coffers for compensation to owners of land no longer required, plus the cost of carrying all their plans through Parliament, and, because of the terrain, the section which had been constructed would have proved expensive. Coupled with this, the company was experiencing opposition from wealthy landowners on the Harpenden section, particularly the Earl of Verulam (although he later relented). Despite the fact that only £15,600 (of the £170,000 authorised) share capital had been raised, with its usual optimism the company, in October 1867, served more compulsory purchase orders, but this was followed by yet another period of inactivity.

By November 1867 the Boxmoor Trustees' patience was wearing thin. An unconnected railway embankment disfigured their Moor and still they were owed compensation. To resolve the matter the Trustees filed a Bill in Chancery on 20th November, 1867 in the suit of 'Cranstone *v.* The Hemel Hempsted & L.N.W.R. Company', claiming £1,413 19*s.* 9*d.*, being the balance of purchase money over and above the Bond paid previously, together with interest at 5 per cent per annum from the time of their taking possession of the land.

Instead of answering the Bill, the Hemel company put in a Demurrer to the effect that the Plaintiffs should have filed the Bill in the name of all the Trustees (any excuse!). The case came to court on Monday 10th February, 1868, when Vice Chancellor Malins found the Demurrer insufficient and gave the company a fortnight to prepare its evidence. At the final hearing it was stated 'the Defendants have in their possession divers documents relating to the subject matter of this suit whereby the truth would appear but they refuse to produce same'. The Hemel company lost, and was ordered to pay over the balance of purchase monies, plus costs, within 14 days. In fact the company settled on 28th May, together with £280 2*s.* 6*d.* interest.

The company was also in debt to the canal company, which in May 1869 instructed a Mr Rogers to call upon the railway company to pay for 17 perches of land, for which only a deposit of £50 had been paid.

Meanwhile, in 1868, two things happened which gave the company new heart. An announcement on 28th July that a new gasworks was to be built on land 'by the new railway bridge at Boxmoor' opened up a possibility of coal traffic using its line, but even more important, Parliament passed the Regulation of Railways Act, and under this Act the Hemel company applied for a Board of Trade Licence to operate its line as a light railway, permission for which was granted on 26th June, 1869. This put some limitation on the running of the line insofar as speed restriction and size of locomotive were concerned, but in its favour was the ability to build sharper curves and steeper gradients. In anticipation of a Licence being granted, the company appointed Mr Ambrose Oliver as contractor for the extension, and by June 1869 his men had fenced off another stretch of the Moor.

Putting all these things together, it would appear that at last the Hemel company had something positive with which to re-approach the LNWR. With the line progressing at such slow speed there was no danger of competition from the Midland or Great Northern companies, and a new gasworks needing coal was a tempter just around the corner from the LNWR station. From the Hemel company's own point of view, a connection at Boxmoor could enable a section from there to Hemel Hempstead town to be operated, creating a most welcome income.

To this end a plan was prepared and signed by Grover, dated 5th March,

1869, which shows the Hemel Hempstead line built as far as Roughdown Road bridge (at the end of the LNWR goods yard). It details various connections in and around the goods yard and appears to indicate that at last the two companies were agreeing to do business, since it is coloured up to show each company's financial liability. The LNWR was to be responsible for providing a new trailing point from its up goods line onto a new section of the Hemel Hempstead line, plus a new point to connect that line to the coal yard sidings, which would involve building a new span for Roughdown Road bridge. The Hemel company was to pay for a short length of double track between the two sets of points. Bearing in mind the date of the plan, it is possible that, a) it was a proposal used as part of the Hemel company's case for a Light Railway Licence, or b) that a working arrangement between the two companies was being negotiated. Or both.

A major breakthrough came at an LNWR Way & Works Committee Meeting on 21st October, 1869, when Mr Wood reported an agreed Easement between the two companies in the sum of £150 (to be paid in advance before possession was given) and an annual sum of £10 was suggested for use of the sidings 'in the rear of or through the coal wharf so long as the L.N.W. permit the use of such sidings'. Although the principle of a connection had been accepted, there was no provision for passenger accommodation on Grover's plan, insofar as LNWR rails were concerned. However, if that plan was the one on which this agreement was based, then it would have been possible for the Hemel company to build its own station/halt on its own side of Roughdown Road bridge.

Having settled the Boxmoor Trust, virtually agreed terms with the LNWR and seeing contractors working on the line, John Grover must have felt that, at long last, his efforts were bearing fruit. The local press, however, were still sceptical: 'The new Railway - This affair is progressing. It moves, certainly, but very slowly. The younger portion of our rising generation, should they live to a good old age, may perhaps see the permanent way completed.' Even if his Hemel Hempstead project caused him some pain, at least Grover could delight in one personal achievement when the pier at Clevedon, Somerset, which he engineered, was completed in 1869.

Despite the newspaper's gloomy prediction, it seems Mr Oliver's men had set about their task immediately and earnestly because by mid-November 1869 work on the three-arch bridge over Lower Marlowes and the River Gade was well under way. Being the largest item of construction on the whole extension, it had been necessary to erect a tremendous amount of scaffolding, which partially blocked the roadway below. So incensed was Mr F.J. Moore, Chairman of Hemel Hempstead Magistrates, when he discovered that horse-drawn vehicles were unable to pass and must go via Cotterells (which he described as a ploughed field) that he took out a Summons against Mr Oliver on 11th November, 1869 for obstructing the highway.

Railway construction was often accompanied by human suffering, which was hardly surprising considering the nature of the navvies' work, and the Hemel Hempstead project was no exception. In November 1869 Shadrack Rising, who was tip-driving on the Moor, stumbled and fell under the wheels of a truck, severing his toes. He was taken to West Herts Infirmary, where 'he progressed

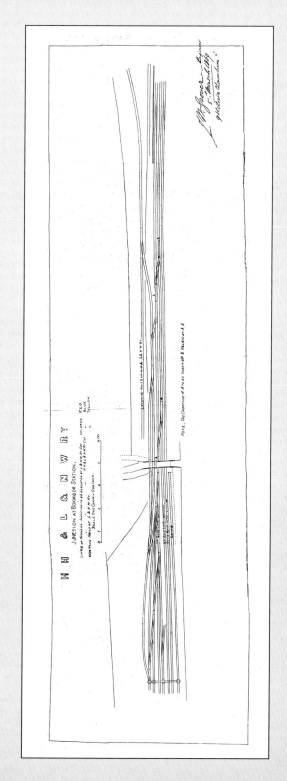

Plan of proposed layout for a junction linking the Hemel Hempstead branch with LNWR main line at Boxmoor station. These proposals, dated 5th March, 1869, were not acted upon.

well'. In trouble for his own sins was navvy William Smith, who on 24th December, 1869 was fined £1, plus £1 4s. (or 21 days in prison), for being quarrelsome and drunk.

The most serious accident happened at 4 pm on 5th January, 1870, when William Eames (22) and James Bradford (28) were killed under a landslip in a 17 ft deep cutting which was being dug in Mr Jagger's field (behind Marlowes). Earth slipped from about 7 ft up and it took 1½ hours to dig out their bodies, with that of George Eames (brother) who had survived in an air pocket under a plank. The surgeon to the men working on the line, G.P. Bernard, told the inquest they had died of suffocation (there were no wounds or breaks). A recovered Shadrack Rising also gave evidence and the jury returned a verdict of 'Accidental Death'.

The two men were laid to rest at Bourne End. Bradford had been a member of the Berkshire Lodge of Oddfellows and about 150 members of the Lodge preceded the coffins, wearing their usual funeral attire. In addition, an estimated crowd of 2,000 witnessed the burials, including many employed on the new railway.

Grover's determination to see the railway progress beyond Hemel Hempstead town is proved by his dealings with Mr Shadrack Godwin of Grove Hill, Hemel Hempstead. Compulsory purchase orders had been dispatched on 12th June, 1869, in response to which Mr Godwin had demanded a very inflated price for his land, and by February 1870 no firm agreement existed between the two parties. A meeting between Mr Barlow (for the company) and Mr Godwin, at which plans, sections and details of a new bridge were considered, failed to assuage the gentleman, and the desperation of the whole situation is well illustrated by the following letter from Grover, dated 24th March, 1870, to his uncle, Mr C.E. Grover, the local solicitor:

I do not know whether your firm is acting for Mr Godwin or not. I believe you are - anyhow I write a friendly letter not as Engineer of this undertaking but simply as a friend and one who has taken a considerable deal of trouble in evidencing the undertaking (very foolishly no doubt). Mr Godwin's claim, with accommodation works, amounts to over £4,000 for under 6 acres of arable land. To state the figure is sufficient. This money will either not be available or if it is the line will not be made. The practical effect of the classic is this - we cannot get another shilling subscribed for works beyond the town, so there the line must, and will stop. I have done my very best to avert it and have endeavoured to raise money in every conceivable channel during the last few weeks, but in the face of the outrageous demands not only are the original promoters driven away but others cannot be found. No doubt Mr Godwin thinks there is a Bond at the Treasury but the amount of that now liable is so trifling as not to affect the position.

I think it only fair to let you know these facts in confidence and hope you will communicate these to Mr Godwin also confidentially. He is, and will be, together with your town, the greatest sufferer by the abandonment of the undertaking. Believe me, my dear Uncle,

Your affectionate nephew,
J.W.G.

This letter drew no immediate solution, but by May 1870 the Hemel company was planning to cut costs by an alteration of line and levels over Mr Godwin's land, reducing what was to have been a 27 ft deep cutting to only 4 ft. This upset Mr Godwin who complained he would suffer noise and annoyance from the trains.

Despondency was all around. The time allowed for building to be completed had expired and the money had run out. Landowners were making it impossible to advance beyond Hemel Hempstead and so the company was left with only one alternative - to apply for an extension of time for two years and apply to the LNWR to implement the agreed plan, in order that a short line would at least be completed between Hemel Hempstead and Boxmoor. The extension of time was granted on 11th October, 1870 and on 17th February, 1871 a letter from Mr Butler was read at an LNWR Special Committee Meeting, requesting permission to form the connection in Boxmoor Coal Yard. The matter was referred to the General Manager and permission granted, but yet another problem awaited the company.

This concerned the Hemel company's Parliamentary Agent, Mr Henry Moon. On 28th January, 1868, having not been paid for his work on the 1863 and 1866 Acts, he had sued the company for £1,000 in respect of work done and materials provided. At the hearing on 21st July, 1868 he was awarded costs of £238 8s. 11d. and £30 1s. 1d., plus £30 12s. and £17 10s., being the costs of bringing the Bills to Parliament, plus newspaper advertisements. Not surprisingly, the company failed to pay up, and probably considered the matter closed when Mr Moon died.

His widow, Sarah Moon, however, had other ideas and on 18th February, 1869 resurrected the claim, again without success. On 5th December, 1870 the Sheriff of Herts was given a writ to serve on the Hemel company 'to take goods, chattels and effects belonging to the said Company' in an effort to settle the claim by value of goods rather than money, but he was unable to gain access to the company and could therefore claim nothing. This was the final straw for Mrs Moon, who applied for the abandonment of the line and in evidence on 3rd May, 1871 she said there had never been any traffic on the line and no works had been done there 'for a long space of time past'. This was not quite true but it had the desired effect and, threatened with abandonment, the company settled the claim on 19th May.

In fact by this time the company had constructed its access into Boxmoor goods yard, via a new wide arch to Roughdown Road bridge (of totally different construction from the original bridge). The Hemel line ran through the arch before dividing into a loop which ran for approximately 100 yards through the goods area, followed by a short spur on which was a turntable connection with the LNWR sidings.

Having averted one disaster, another now befell the company. John Barrow, who had supported the infant scheme and backed it at every stage of its development (including financial support) died in July 1871, aged 82, after a lingering illness. As luck would have it, Barrow's son, John James Barrow, decided to take up where his father had left off and with his arrival came a new approach all round. The Hemel Hempstead company's Board, which had formerly comprised local businessmen, suddenly consisted of out-of-town people - supposedly people of influence where it was needed.

Chapter Three

The Third Act

By 1871 the line was built between Boxmoor and Queensway. Work was in progress from Queensway to Cupid Green and the route staked out as far as Wood End. Then the new Board had new ideas! They prepared yet another plan, and another Bill for Parliament to consider. This plan was deposited with the Clerk of the Peace on 9th November, 1871 and received approval on 18th July, 1872. This new Act contained a bold proposal to extend the line through Boxmoor goods yard, with the Hemel company buiding its own station adjacent to the entrance to Boxmoor station. Also mentioned was a further plan signed by Grover and Henry Oakley of the GNR, so the Hemel company had still not entirely abandoned the idea of obtaining a connection in that direction.

Again compulsory purchase powers were given for three years, with completion in four years in respect of the new parts, and three years for those parts covered by the 1866 Act. A 5 per cent deposit of £105 was paid in respect of the new works at Boxmoor and the Tolls listed in the 1863 Act were repealed in favour of new ones set out at length, covering passenger and freight charges. The company had hinted at providing a station for Mr Godwin's use, but his response came through his solicitor, that he 'would only be expected to pay a toll to use it'!

Permission to alter certain levels, allowing 1 in 40 gradients instead of 1 in 60 was allowed by the Act, together with a deviation of about 1 mile 3 furlongs, with steeper gradients between Adeyfield Road and Three Cherry Trees Lane, terminating in a field belonging to Lady Glamis.

During 1872 the company continued to exchange correspondence with Mr Godwin concerning those parts of his land which they wished to purchase. Eventually, after making many suggestions and stipulations, an agreement was reached, a) to lower the line, thus avoiding a hump-backed bridge (and supposedly reducing the noise of the trains), b) to erect substantial fences to keep in Godwin's animals and c) to pay him compensation for loss of timber and growing crops.

The Hemel company also accepted responsibility for Godwin's legal and surveyors' fees and agreed to 'make and manage' a proper siding at High Street Green, mainly for Godwin's use. Finalisation of these conditions was expected on or before 26th August, 1872, but Godwin asked for signing to be delayed so that he could harvest his crops, which were only a week away from ripening. The company took possession of his land early in September, following a payment of £1,400 'on account' and £52 10s. to Sedgwick & Son, Godwin's surveyors.

It was during 1872 that the development of this railway became the focus of attention for some newly interested parties. During the time the last Bill was travelling through Parliament secret advances were made by Hemel company Board member, Alexander Clunes Sherriff, MP, to the Midland Railway Company's General Manager, Mr James Allport. At a meeting of the Midland

Board on 1st May, 1872 a letter was read, asking whether that company would enter into negotiations for working the Hemel Hempstead railway when completed. Allport was authorised to give the matter some consideration and report back to the Board. This he did on 5th June, and it was resolved 'that no agreement be entered into other than an agreement for working the line at 50 per cent of the gross receipts'. A Midland Consultation Committee Meeting on 3rd July suggested to the Board a working agreement on the following terms:

1.   The line be completed to the satisfaction of the MR Engineers.
2.   The line be worked by the Midland who shall be allowed 50 per cent of the gross receipts for working expenses after the usual deductions have been provided for, and
3.   The MR to guarantee in perpetuity 4½ per cent on a capital not exceeding £65,000.

After discussion, it was resolved to simplify the terms and offer the Hemel company £3,500 annual rental for their line.

The following day Mr Allport reported that he had met Mr Sherriff, who had stated his inability to raise capital for the line on the terms originally proposed by the Midland, but that he would undertake to complete the line to the reasonable satisfaction of the Midland Engineer and hand it over to the Midland company at a fixed rental of £3,750 pa. It was resolved to recommend to the next Board Meeting acceptance of this offer, if made with all necessary and suitable conditions. This offer was duly confirmed on 16th July, 1872, just two days before the new Act was passed by Parliament.

It should be remembered that no matter how satisfactory this deal was for the Midland company and Mr Sherriff, he had nevertheless acted in secrecy and still had to confront his own company. On doing so he met with mixed reactions. On the one hand they had at last found a company prepared to work with them, but on the other hand the terms were considered unacceptable. Despite this, their hands were very firmly tied and there was no alternative other than to accept Sherriff's agreement. From then on all reference to the Great Northern connection was dropped and efforts were started to plan a junction with the Midland main line near Harpenden.

In pre-commuter days priority was given to obtaining the best trade routes, so in this case Luton was obviously more beneficial than Harpenden, necessitating a north-bound junction. Luton was the centre of hat manufacture (particularly straw hats) and although factories imported vast quantities of straw plait, they still needed locally produced plait, consequently Hemel Hempstead's plaiters would certainly benefit from this rail link. There was also the added attraction of obtaining cheaper coal through the Midland Railway system.

Without further ado the Hemel company applied in December 1872 to acquire a piece of Midland land on which to create its junction, a request which was passed to Mr Gratton and the Way & Works Committee. Long deliberations and negotiations followed, during which time Grover went off to Venezuela in 1873 to carry out surveys for a mountain railway from La Guaira to Caracas, and also for a new harbour scheme. It is on record that when he returned he gave up railway works in this country and turned to waterworks. However, he maintained his link with the Hemel Hempstead line right up to opening day.

By this time building work at the Hemel Hempstead end had reached Highfield Lane bridge and a new contractor, Mr Scott, was employed. Land required at Redbourn had been staked out but the company was encountering difficulties with Lady Glamis over a piece of land valued by her at £2,400, for which the company had offered only £886 0s. 4d. in compensation. The Directors set about summoning a jury to decide upon a reasonable amount of compensation and a warrant was received at 2.30 pm on 9th January, 1873, a copy of which still exists and bears the Seal of the Hemel Hempsted & L.N.W. Railway Company. The case was heard on 29th January, 1873 by Thomas Curtis, Sheriff of Hertfordshire; the jury decided on compensation of £437 10s. for one lot 'free from incumbrance' and £650 for the other 'by way of compensation for the damage to be sustained by reason of the severing thereof from other lands of the owners'.

Never long out of trouble, the Hemel company received complaints from the Hemel Hempstead authorities about the state of the road bridge at Cupid Green, to which they replied that they were doing all in their power to improve the road. In January 1873 another complaint was made, this time relating to the road surface under the bridge at Heath Park (Boxmoor). During construction a spring was discovered here that kept the road wet. The water table was high and occasionally the cellar of the nearby Heath Park Hotel became flooded. The railway company raised the path under the bridge, but by 1876 the Council was still complaining, so to remedy the situation the spring was blocked up, but this met with public disapproval, so much so that in 1883 it was opened up again!

The sad state of the Hemel company's financial situation was evident from its Statement of Accounts for the half-year ending on 31st December, 1873, which was put before the Half-Yearly General Meeting of Shareholders on Friday 27th February, 1874.

Of the £170,000 shares created by the 1866 Act only £15,600's worth had been sold and the company had a cash balance in the bank of only £172 19s. 6d. It was surviving on temporary loans totalling £58,068 0s. 3d. - thus the company was 'in the red' to the extent of £57,895 0s. 9d.

By this time the company had expended a total of £93,025 0s. 9d. on the project, and during the previous half-year a total of £24,914 11s. 1d. had been spent, made up as follows:

	£	s.	d.
Land Purchase and Compensation	836	10	7
Works	23,837	0	8
Engineering	100	0	0
Law and Parliamentary, etc.	140	19	10

However, a note stated 'no reliable estimate of further expenditure on capital account can be given at present' and another proclaimed 'the Company has no rolling stock'. In truth it did not have much of anything and desperately needed the support of the Midland Railway to achieve its aim.

The Directors of the Hemel company must have heaved a huge sigh of relief, therefore, on 20th January, 1874, when the Midland agreed to grant, in the sum of £100, an Easement on to its main line at Harpenden, together with the use of two pieces of Midland land, providing the Hemel company obtained and handed over to it another suitable piece of land, which together could provide sidings at the junction.

Despite this more delays followed, during which emerged the reality of Mr Sherriff's secret negotiations; the line was taking much longer to build than anticipated and thus the rental was quite unrealistic. The company therefore wrote to Allport, advising him that Sherriff had not been authorised to arrange leasing the line and demanding better terms. In a swift reply Allport asked if the Midland were 'now free of all involvement in the line' - in other words, take it or leave it! This obviously frightened the Directors of the Hemel company who immediately ordered their solicitor, Mr Forster, to contact Mr Allport and after much correspondence the Midland Board decided, at a meeting on 7th October, 1874, to confirm its willingness to work the line on the terms already agreed.

With this matter finally resolved the subject of the junction was re-opened and plans drawn up. The Midland company agreed to pay for the work to be done on its line and the Hemel company was expected to pay the rest. In fact an Estimate of £3,460 was submitted to the Midland Way & Works Committee on 6th July, 1875, which passed it to the General Purposes Committee, where it was sanctioned, the cost to be charged to capital.

Meanwhile, heartened by its progress, the Hemel company placed the following advertisement in the *Railway Times* on 19th June, 1875:

Tenders invited for the erection of Stations at Hemel Hempstead and Redbourn, earthworks and laying out of station yards, sidings and various other works necessary for the completion of this railway, 9 miles in length. Plans and Specifications can be seen at the offices of J.W. GROVER, Esq., C.E., Westminster on and after 16th June between 10 am and 4 pm and tenders for the work will require to be lodged with the Secretary of the Company, marked 'Tender for Works' not later than 26th June. The Directors do not bind themselves to accept the lowest or any tender. By Order of the Board,
Rod. Mackay, Secretary,
2nd June, 1875

Construction had reached Redbourn, by January 1875, at which point the line was crossed by a public footpath. Grover wrote to the Clerk of St Albans Highways Board and they arranged to meet on site at an early date, presumably to determine the kind of crossing to be provided. Their decisions are unknown, but the company's eventual actions certainly failed to meet the approval of Redbourn residents, 50 of whom signed a petition which was forwarded to the Highways Board by Mr Roberts, Waywarden of Redbourn, in March 1876.

It read as follows:

We, the undersigned ratepayers of the parish of Redbourn, desire to direct your attention to the inconvenience and loss we have sustained by the destruction of the footpath by the L.N.W. & H.H. Rly. Co. This path was much used by labourers going to and from their work. We think that a footbridge should be put across and over the railway, and that such a bridge should be in every respect a convenient one to use. We therefore beg your honourable Board to take such steps as will compel the aforesaid railway company to provide us the means of using the footpath of which we are at present deprived.

The Highways Clerk was directed to acknowledge receipt of the memorial and write to the 'LNWR Co.'. If he did write to that company, rather than the HH & LNWR Co., that would account for the fact that he never received a reply! Certainly, a footbridge was not provided - but the problem did not go away.

By January 1876 the Hemel company was in a predicament, being tied to the Midland by a less than satisfactory leasing arrangement, which had not then been sealed and settled, and unable to raise much-needed cash by selling off surplus land, because that had been claimed by the Midland as part of its interest in the scheme. On 15th January Mr Godwin's solicitors wrote to the Hemel company in an effort to acquire some of the surplus land, but the company replied the following day that it would be 'much better to leave the whole question of surplus land until completion of the line'. Bravely, it struggled on, hoping to have the line open by May - only to have those hopes dashed too.

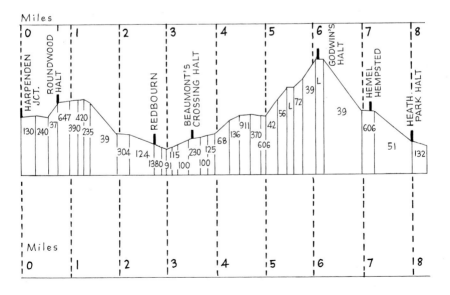

Gradient Profile

Chapter Four

Deflation and Elation

Although the line was virtually complete, it was not signalled. Rather reluctantly the Midland agreed to carry out the work at an estimated cost of £1,500 (to be paid by the local company) and on 16th May, 1876 it was reported that the Midland Engineer had received £500 towards this cost. Accordingly they resolved to carry out £500's worth of signalling work, and no more. Whether or not the Hemel company ever managed to raise the remaining £1,000 is open to question, but it seems more likely that the Midland took pity on them in an effort to get the line operational. On 16th June, 1876 Mr Mackay, Company Secretary to the Hemel company, wrote to the Board of Trade asking for their requirements in regard to lines about to be opened to traffic, and stating the line would be ready for inspection at the end of July.

His optimism was misplaced, because on 11th August Grover wrote to the Midland Engineer requesting him to visit the line before the contractors left, with a view to ensuring they had 'complied with his wishes in respect of work which was incomplete when he last visited it'. Ever cautious, the matter was referred to the Board for instructions, discussed at meetings on 6th September and 4th October, but eventually permission was given for an inspection.

Meanwhile, without waiting for Midland consent, the Hemel company wrote to the Board of Trade giving notice that the line would be ready for 'the safe conveyance of passengers on 30th September' and asking for an inspection at any time during the 10 days after that date. Col William Yolland, the Inspector, agreed to visit the line on 6th October, but due to Mr Mackay's absence in the north of England the matter was not brought to the attention of the Hemel Directors until it was too late to make the necessary arrangements.

On 7th October Yolland wrote to Mackay saying that he had received details of the line from Grover, in which it was stated the Midland company was in the process of putting up signals. Yolland, therefore, agreed to inspect on Wednesday, 25th October, on condition that all works and signals would by then be complete. As if by way of prior judgement he added, 'I passed the junction in a Midland train the other day and I could not see any shelter on the platform and I therefore mention that I should not pass the line if such shelter had not been provided'. This drew an immediate response - that as no trains would be stopping at the junction, no shelter would be required (a platform had been provided for construction materials only).

In order to make his inspection, Yolland had requested a special train from St Pancras about 9 am, or other suitable arrangements to get him to the line, and the company was required to make provision for testing deflections of the girder bridges under a rolling load. Col Yolland duly left St Pancras at 9.10 am on 25th October on a special train and made his inspection, after which officials of both companies joined in a luncheon at Hemel Hempstead station. As it turned out, there was little to celebrate as Col Yolland was not impressed by the line, as his report shows:

I have the honor to report for the information of the Board of Trade in compliance with the instructions contained in your Minute of the 25th ultimo, that I have inspected the Hemel Hempstead & London & North Western Railway, which is single throughout. Its length is 7 miles 34½ chains. There is also a portion of goods line from Hemel Hempstead to Boxmoor Station on the LNW. This line joins the up and down lines of the Midland Railway at Harpenden Junction between the 25½ and 25¾ mile posts from London. The width of the line at formation level is firm, 18 to 19 feet on embankments and 15 feet in cuttings. There are sidings at Hemel Hempstead and Redbourn stations and also at what is called Godwin's siding, but there are not passing places. The land has been purchased for a double line if hereafter required but the works at present are only for a single line.

The gauge of the railway is 4 feet 8½ inches - the permanent way consists of a double headed iron rail, which weighs 60 lb. per linear yard in lengths of 24 feet, fixed in cast iron chairs that each weigh 26 lb., by means of wooden keys placed outside the rails. The chairs are fastened to cross sleepers by means of 2 wrought iron twisted spikes to each chair. The joints of the rails are fixed in the usual manner. The sleepers are of red fir, 8 feet 11 inches long, by 9 inches x 4½ inches rectangular, laid 2 feet apart at the joints but they average 3 feet apart for the 24 feet rail. The ballast is of good gravel and is stated to be 8 inches in depth below the sleepers. The steepest gradient on the line has an inclination of 1 in 40 and the sharpest curve has a radius of 10 chains.

There are 15 bridges on the line, 7 over and 8 under. Two of the over bridges are constructed of timber, and the remainder of brick in which the largest span slightly exceeds 14 feet. Of the under bridges, these are constructed wholly of brick and the remaining five have brick abutments and wrought iron girders. Among the latter, the largest span is 37 feet on the skew. The iron girder bridges have sufficient theoretical strength and exhibited moderate deflections under a rolling load. The line is in fair order but there have been slight slips in the cuttings which require clearing up.

In going over the line I noticed the following requirements:

1. The sharp curve of 10 chains radius requires a check rail.
2. At 5 m. 54 chains both abutments and wing walls of an under bridge having wrought iron girders are very defective. The abutments are not vertical and there are extensive cracks on each side. It may require to be wholly or partially rebuilt. The arch of another under bridge of 30 feet span built in brick at 0.50 m. 3 chains exhibits a longitudinal crack of considerable length. The crack may probably be prevented from extending by means of tie rods through the piers over the spandrils.
3. The junction at Harpenden on the Midland Railway had not been completed and the points and signals were not in all cases connected together, and some of the facing points at the stations require locking bars.
4. No engine turntables have been provided - one is required at each extremity of the passenger line, or the 2nd one will suffice to be at the station on the Midland line from whence the passenger traffic is to be worked by that Company.
5. Provision has not been made for working the traffic on the absolute block system.
6. The points leading to a ballast pit near Redbourne must be taken out, or if suffered to remain in, they must be properly protected. The fencing is incomplete at the same place.
7. Clocks will be required to face the platforms at Hemel Hempstead and Redbourn station and in the signal boxes. Godwin's siding can be safely used as long as only one train is permitted to be on the line.
8. An undertaking will be required as to the mode of working which is intended to be adopted. This must be given by the Company which has constructed the line and be concurred in by the Midland Railway Co., which is, I understand, to work it.

The delay in making this inspection has been due to a request from the Secretary of the Company. I have now therefore to report that by reason of the incompleteness of the works, the opening of the Hemel Hempstead & London & North Western Railway cannot be sanctioned without danger to the Public using the same. I have the honor to be, your most obedient servant, Yolland.

How dejected the Hemel Directors must have been - rebuilding a bridge and providing turntables required extra finance, and they could certainly not be provided in the statutory month allowed for faults to be rectified. Somehow, though, they were able to convince the Midland Engineer (who had been present at the inspection) that if the Midland company would do the work the local company would pay for it. When this was reported to the Midland Board on 1st November it was agreed that an estimate be prepared and when (and only when!) the Hemel company produced the money the work would be executed.

However, anticipating that opening could not be too far away, the Midland Board looked again at the terms drawn up in principle concerning the working of the branch and on 1st December, 1876 a formal Agreement was concluded, the terms of which were as follows:

1. So soon as the line has received the authority of the Board of Trade to be opened for public traffic, the Midland Company shall immediately and for ever afterwards at their own expense maintain, renew, manage, stock, work and use the new line, shall have the sole right of fixing charges, etc., and shall indemnify the Hemel Company from and against all actions, claims and demands whatsoever in respect of the maintenance and working of the line.
2. The Midland Company shall pay and shall indemnify the Hemel Company against all expenses of management, taxes, rates, etc. except rent charges for land on which the line is constructed.
3. The Hemel Hempstead Company shall be entitled to retain or sell superfluous lands adjoining the new line.
4. The Midland Company shall pay to the Hemel Company:
   a) For the half year or portion of a half year ending 30th June or the 31st December next after the new line shall have been opened for public traffic a sum bearing such proportion of £3,750 as the period during which the new line shall have been opened bears to a year.
   b) For each subsequent half year ending 30th June or 31st December the sum of £1,875.
5. The sums payable under the last article shall be paid within one month. In the event of default interest to be paid at 5 per cent.
6. Agreement to be sanctioned by Parliament at the cost of the Midland Company, supported by the Hemel Company.
7. Any difference of opinion between the two companies to be settled by arbitration.

A sigh of relief must have greeted this signed and sealed Agreement, but each month brought a postponement notice from the Board of Trade, each being acknowledged by Mackay with the same promise - that they 'will push on with the completion of those requirements by every means in their power'. Fate did not help, though, for on 15th February, 1877 the new signal box built by the Midland to control working on the branch was extensively damaged by fire, caused by an overheated stove pipe.

At a meeting of the Midland Locomotive Department, on 6th March, 1877, consideration was given to an estimate of £102 10s. for providing a 3,500 gallon water tank, sand furnace, and washing out apparatus at Hemel Hempstead, so that an engine could be kept there. This proposal was passed to the General Purposes Committee for approval.

Following receipt of the March postponement notice Mackay informed the Board of Trade that he was expecting any day to hear that work on the line was complete, they were only waiting to hear from the Midland 'who are doing some of the work'. The Midland company, meanwhile, had been doing some homework on the subject of turntables and (no doubt mindful of the expense of installing one) wrote the following letter to the Board of Trade:

29th March 1877
When the government inspector was over the Hemel Hempstead line he suggested the necessity for an engine turntable at Hemel Hempstead and at Luton, to and from which place the trains for the branch will run.

I am aware a deputation saw the President of the BOT respecting the question of providing engine turntables generally but more particularly with regard to a London North Western case at Newry [?]. I believe the requirement for the engine turntable at Newry was waived, but the general question was to stand over until a meeting had been held between the companies and the officers of the BOT. Pending this meeting it does not appear desirable that we should provide a turntable at Luton, as the branch will be worked with a tank engine and I shall be glad to know that our not doing so, subject of course to what is ultimately decided upon, would not prevent the BOT sanctioning the opening of the Hemel Hempstead branch after the requirements particularly relating to it of Col Yolland are complied with. Will you kindly let me hear from you whether I am correct in this conclusion?

After due consideration, the Board of Trade replied on 9th April to confirm that the Midland could proceed towards the opening of the line, pending the outcome of the turntable deliberations. However, within days the Midland Company was instructed to provide a turntable at Luton and dealt with it as a matter of urgency. (This was inspected on 18th September, 1877. On the same day the new engine shed and water tank at Hemel Hempstead were also visited and approved.)

With this position clarified, the Hemel company was able to give notice to the BOT on 19th April that the line would be ready for inspection as from 21st April, and on 20th April Grover wrote to Yolland requesting him to visit the line on either 25th or 27th April. As neither date was convenient, Yolland suggested Thursday, 3rd May. Accordingly Mackay telegraphed Allport to arrange for a special train from St Pancras. Allport then telegraphed Yolland to alter the date to 4th May.

So it was that on Friday 4th May, 1877, Col Yolland arrived at Harpenden with an inspection party comprising Mr Johnson, Engineer of the Midland Railway, Mr Needham, Midland's general superintendent of lines, Mr Grover, Mr Smedley, Mr Scott, the contractor and Mr Campbell, resident Engineer and superintendent of the Hemel line. Anticipating Yolland's approval, a champagne luncheon had been arranged, catered for by Mr Watkins of the Kings Arms Hotel, Hemel Hempstead.

Yolland's second report read as follows:

I have the honor to report for the information of the BOT in compliance with the instructions contained in your Minute of 21st ultimo, that I have reinspected the Hemel Hempstead & LNWR between Harpenden Junction on the Midland Railway, 4½ miles south of Luton station, and Hemel Hempstead. I had in the first instance proposed to make this reinspection on the 25th ult. but postponed it, in consequence of the inability of the engineer of the Midland Railway Company (who are to work the line) to attend at that time. The requirements detailed in my report of inspection of the 27th October, 1876 have now been attended to with the exception which I shall mention -

The Hemel Hempstead & LNWR have provided and set up an engine turntable at Hemel Hempstead and the Midland Railway Company have provided an engine turntable, and have let the contract for its erection at Luton (from whence the traffic to and from Hemel Hempstead is to be worked) and the work is in hand, and expected to be completed in about a month. A pair of facing points 9 feet in length, leading into Godwin's siding are to be replaced by a pair of facing points 12 feet in length.

My attention was drawn to the fact that the statutory height of 15 feet had not been provided at the under bridge over a public road at 5 miles 54 chains, the heights being 13 ft 10 in. on the upper side and 14 ft 1 in. on the lower side. This was stated to have been done at the request of the local authorities. If any question should hereafter be raised on the subject, the Hemel Hempstead Company will make the alteration required in the level of the road to provide the statutory height.

A question was also raised whether a road crossed on the level at about 3 miles 33 chains (Harpendenbury) was a public carriage road or not. It is returned in the details as a private road and footpath, but it has more the appearance of a public road and a man in the employ of the Company who was on duty at it stated that it was a public road, with a right of way for all vehicles, but in opposition to this statement it was also mentioned that it was kept in repair by the owner of an adjacent property. I have no means of ascertaining whether it is a public or a private road but the Superintendent of the Midland Railway said that it would be necessary to place a box there, and station a man at it, and probably ultimately to build a cottage for a platelayer, whose wife would attend to the gates. These gates had padlocks on them for the day and the man had the key but the padlocks would be removed at night.

In accordance therefore with the terms of the letter from the BOT to the General Manager of the Midland Railway, dated 9th April, 1877, I have now to state that there will be no objection to the opening of the Hemel Hempstead & LNW Railway as soon as a satisfactory undertaking has been received as to the mode of working the traffic on the line. I understand it is to be worked on the train staff and ticket system or to have only one engine on the line, combined with the absolute block system, and that no two trains are to be on the line between Hemel Hempstead and Redbourn Station at one and the same time in order to avoid the risk attendant on any vehicle breaking away at Godwin's Siding.

The luncheon which followed was a much happier affair, with Grover proposing a toast 'Success to the Hemel Hempstead Railway under the management of the Midland Railway Company', and declaring that Hemel Hempstead would be found to be a good town which would contribute its share towards repaying the cost and trouble expended on the line. Mr Johnson replied on behalf of the Midland company.

Chapter Five

Success at Last!

The day after Yolland's inspection Mackay wrote to the BOT asking if there were any specific forms to be completed for the opening of a single line railway, and could he have three copies. On 7th May the BOT sent him a copy of Yolland's report and informed him there was no special form, but that details of working should be set down under the Seals of both companies. On 29th May Mackay sent the undertaking but this was returned because it did not comply with the last paragraph of Yolland's report.

An amended letter of undertaking was sent on 6th June and on 9th June the company received the letter it had waited so long for - 'The undertaking is satisfactory and the BOT have no objection to the opening of the railway for passenger traffic on condition that it shall be worked in accordance therewith'.

However, there was no provision for a passenger service between the town of Hemel Hempstead and Boxmoor station and public feelings were voiced by a newspaper editorial:

> Nothing could be more absurd than the inability of the Midland and North Western to arrange a connection between their systems, by means of the line which has already been constructed across the Moor; jealousy is understandable but why should passengers suffer?

Another editorial referred to the 'half-completed junction' at Boxmoor as a 'perpetual monument to the power of self interest and prejudice'!

At the 'eleventh hour' the Midland Railway Company's Engineer announced that he had not been totally satisfied with the way Yolland's requirements had been carried out and, to cover the company, a further Agreement was drawn up, passing back to the Hemel company responsibility for strengthening or rebuilding the bridges at Harpenden (over the turnpike road) and Three Cherry Trees Lane at Hemel Hempstead, should the need arise and for provision of gatekeepers' houses (if needed) at Redbourn (Flowers Farm Crossing) and Harpendenbury.

In order to satisfy Parliamentary requirements, this Agreement, dated 21st June, was hurriedly signed and sealed and, on 10th July, Allport sent provisional timetables and fares to the BOT for approval. By coincidence, BOT approval and Parliamentary consent were obtained on the same day - 12th July, 1877, as a result of which an opening day was set for Monday, 16th July.

This allowed very little time for planning celebrations, but at 5 pm that afternoon the High Bailiff, Mr P. Evilthrift, chaired a preconvened meeting of leading inhabitants in the Town Hall to consider the matter. After some discussion, Mr Stallon (of earlier fame!) proposed a resolution 'that the Directors be asked to provide a train for 150 inhabitants, that the train be applied for by the High Bailiff and that the train follow the 11.10 am train'. This was seconded by Mr G. Smith. Mr Walter Grover counter-proposed that the

HEMEL HEMPSTEAD BAILIWICK,

CELEBRATION OF THE

OPENING OF THE

NEW LINE OF RAILWAY

FROM

Hemel Hempstead to Luton

MONDAY, JULY 16, 1877.

By permission of the Directors and Managers of the Midland Railway Company,

A SPECIAL TRAIN

WILL LEAVE HEMEL HEMPSTEAD FOR LUTON at 11.10 a.m. punctually,

Returning from Luton at 12.40 will be set apart for the accommodation of the High Bailiff and Party, at single Fares for the double Journey

The Inhabitants desirous of commemorating the event are therefore especially invited to meet the HIGH BAILIFF at the TOWN HALL at half-past Ten o'clock a.m., and from thence accompany him over the line, after which, the Directors and Managers of the Line will be entertained by the HIGH BAILIFF, and Inhabitants at a

LUNCHEON in the TOWN HALL

AT HALF-PAST 2 P.M.

As the accommodation by the Train is necessarily limited, early application on the part of Gentlemen intending to accompany the High Bailiff is particularly requested.

Tickets for the Luncheon 4s each, may behad of Mr. Watkins, at the Kings Arms Hotel, Hemel Hempstead of the High Bailiff, and of the Members of the Committee.

F. MASON, MACHINE PRINTER, HEMEL HEMPSTEAD.

Opening day poster.   *Authors' Collection*

Bailiff and his party should go by the very first train at 7.55 am, and Mr Hill seconded. The Bailiff agreed he would 'be happy to accompany anyone wishing to travel on the first train', but when put to the meeting Mr Stallon's resolution was carried by 16 votes to 13. Mr Balderson then proposed that a Committee be appointed to invite the Directors of the railway to a luncheon in the Town Hall on the return of the train from Luton, and to make any other arrangements. This was seconded by Mr Cranstone (the same gentleman who had allowed his name to be used by the Boxmoor Trust when the railway company was sued for non-payment of dues). It was also resolved to allow the High Bailiff £20 to cover incidental expenses.

On 14th July the *Hemel Hempstead Gazette* carried the announcement of the opening. After all the years of watching and waiting, everyone looked forward to the following Monday when their railway would come to life. Not even the dismal weather which arrived with that auspicious day could dampen the enthusiasm and about 100 people, some of whom had arrived at the station at 6 am, witnessed the departure of the very first passenger train, with between 30 and 40 passengers. Most of these returned on the 10.30 am train, in order to say they had travelled by the first train in each direction.

Something of a carnival atmosphere was created as Hemel Hempstead prepared to open its railway. A large canvas banner was stretched across Alexandra Road, proclaiming 'Success to the Hemel Hempstead and Midland Railway Company', the supports of which had been decorated with evergreens. This construction was prepared and erected by Josiah Hales (local plumber, glazier and painter) at a cost of £4 8s. 3d. The day was ushered in by the sound of church bells drifting across the town - swiftly followed by a bill for two guineas!

Many local people assembled with Mr Evilthrift and his under-Bailiff, Mr Solomon Willis, outside the Town Hall and at 10.30 am the procession started towards the station. Due to a prior engagement, the Hemel Hempstead Band (5th Herts) were unable to lead the procession, but their place was ably filled by the Berkhamsted Rifle Corps Band (7th Herts), under the direction of Bandmaster Joseph Pearce. The terms of their hire were a fee of £5, plus dinner and drinks for the 10 musicians.

Just before 11 am the Bailiwick party was met at the station by Mr Needham and other Midland Railway Company representatives, after which they boarded the train of saloon carriages to travel at the special rate of 'single fare for double journey'. At 11.10 am sharp they started smoothly away, amid cheers from onlookers. The train stopped at Godwin's Siding to pick up 'Squire' Godwin and at a very crowded Redbourn station more people hurried on board. It took 20 minutes to reach Redbourn from Hemel Hempstead, and at each waiting place the band entertained.

On arrival at Luton the party, together with the band, made its way in procession through the town, accompanied by the Mayor, Mr Bigg, and most of his Corporation. A visit was made to the Plait Halls and then to the Town Hall, where champagne, sherry and biscuits were served. The Mayor apologised to his guests for the short notice of the visit, and indeed for the short duration of it, which prevented them from receiving their visitors in better form. After

July *14*, 1877.

OPENING OF NEW RAILWAY, FROM HEMEL HEMPSTEAD TO LUTON.

MONDAY, JULY 16, 1877.

———

Sir,—I have to inform you that to celebrate the Opening of the above, A SPECIAL TRAIN, will, by permission of the Midland Railway Company, leave Hemel Hempstead for Luton, at 11.10 a.m. punctually ; returning from Luton at 12.40, will be set apart for the accommodation of the High Bailiff and Party, at Single Fares for the double Journey. The Inhabitants desirous of commemorating the event are therefore especially invited to meet the HIGH BAILIFF at the TOWN HALL, at half-past Ten o'clock, a.m., and from thence accompany him over the line, after which, the Directors and Managers of the Line will be entertained by the HIGH BAILIFF, and Inhabitants at a

LUNCHEON in the TOWN HALL,

At half-past 2 p.m

As the accommodation by the Train is necessarily limited, early application on the part of Gentlemen intending to accompany the HIGH BAILIFF, is particularly requested.

TICKETS for the Luncheon 4s., may be had of Mr. Watkins, of the Kings Arms Hotel, Hemel Hempsted, of the High Bailiff, and of the members of the Committee.

Hoping to be favored with your Company on the occasion.

I am, Sir,
Your Obedient Servant,

PHILIP EVILTHRIFT.

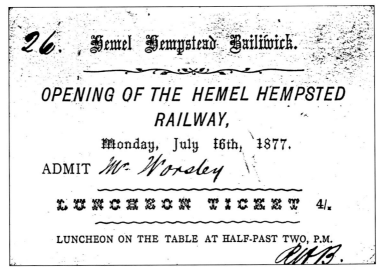

26. Ħemel Ħempstead Bailiwick.

OPENING OF THE HEMEL HEMPSTED RAILWAY,

Monday, July 16th, 1877.

ADMIT *Mr Worsley*

LUNCHEON TICKET 4/.

LUNCHEON ON THE TABLE AT HALF-PAST TWO, P.M.

Luncheon invitation and ticket.

drinking the healths of both Councils the party, including guests from Luton, returned to Luton station, where they were entertained by the Luton Band, before their train departed at 12.40 pm, arriving back in Hemel Hempstead at 1.20 pm.

The Berkhamsted Band played a lively quickstep as it led the assembled company back to the Town Hall, where at 2.30 pm 67 gentlemen, including Mr Renals the new station master, sat down to a cold luncheon 'with many delicacies and champagne', catered for by Mr Watkins of the Kings Arms Hotel, tickets for which had been on public sale, price four shillings each. During the lunch the band played outside, and then retired to the Bell Hotel, along with representatives of the police and sundry others who had assisted in the celebrations. Here they enjoyed a two shilling lunch, washed down with ale and ginger beer.

Following the official lunch, many toasts and speeches were made, and many complimentary words directed towards the Midland Railway Company. John Grover recounted the history of the line, starting with his own proposal for a short line and moving on to the extended line, which had come about as a result of public demand. He even admitted that one of the strongest advocates for the line beyond Hemel Hempstead had been his uncle, Charles Grover! He explained the difficulties which had prolonged its construction, recalling the sight of 'deserted bridges and grass covered tracks'. Completion, he said, was 'a merciful act'.

Alderman Higgins spoke of the benefits the line would bring to the district, linking it with Luton, 'the emporium of the straw trade', and John Barrow Jnr told of his father's involvement with it from the beginning. The Luton visitors returned on the 5.45 pm train, arriving back at 6.22 pm having 'assisted in a very pleasant celebration and one which is likely to be of considerable importance to Luton', according to a Luton newspaper. In all about 300 passengers bought tickets at Hemel Hempstead that first day.

The total cost of the railway was £139,533 9s. 4d., some £50,000 less than the authorised capital of the Acts of 1863 and 1866, and Grover was keen to mention this in his speech as 'perhaps the only example in the country where a line cost less than its estimate'. Whether this was due to careful accounting, corner-cutting or being bailed out by the Midland Railway Company is open to speculation. What we do know, however, is that the organising committee for the opening celebrations overspent by £24 9s. 2d. and to overcome the problem each committee member agreed to contribute £1 8s. from his own pocket!

So, the townsfolk of Hemel Hempstead at last had a railway - but it did not take them to Boxmoor. John Grover had persevered to see his railway open - but it had taken 15 demoralising years of his life. The Barrows, father and son, gave devoted support and financial assistance but gained little satisfaction and, certainly, no reward. The London & North Western Railway Company, for whatever reason, missed out completely but the Midland Railway Company had gained a new line - and they could look forward!

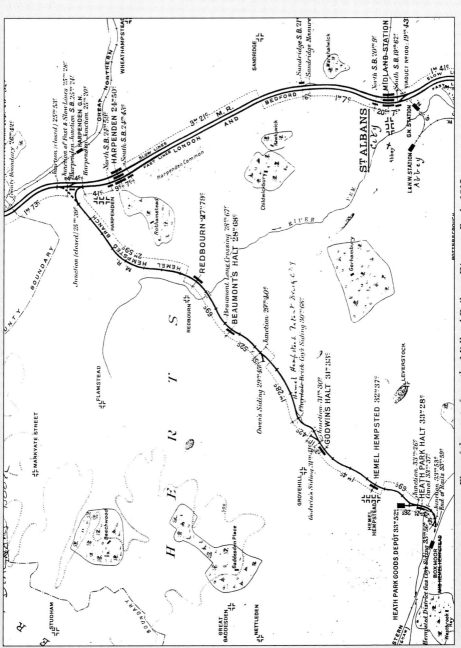

Plan of the route from the Midland Railway Diagram Book, 1912.

Chapter Six

Route

When the branch opened Hemel Hempstead trains commenced their journey at Luton station, stopped at Chiltern Green (to connect with London trains) and then travelled along the Midland main line to the junction on the northern outskirts of Harpenden. Here they ran onto the branch, via a sharp curve, into a cutting and under Ambrose Lane bridge - a brick construction with four arches making up an 88 feet span. This initial stretch of line was abandoned in 1888, when a south-facing curve was installed to take trains out onto the main line and into Harpenden station (*see Chapter Eight*).

Once under Ambrose Lane, the cutting opened out to an embankment and it crossed the turnpike road to Luton (now A1081) by means of a large brick bridge. Because the bridge was built parallel to the railway, the 30 feet wide arch stands at a slight angle to the road. In the east wall is a stone plaque, but any inscription it may have borne has long since been eroded. For some years a postbox was let into the west wall, but in more recent times most of the brickwork has been hidden by advertising hoardings.

This bridge was newly built in May 1875, but was already showing a large crack at the time of Yolland's first inspection in 1876. However, the tie rods he recommended still appear to be holding it together, well over a century later. Because the bridge was built wide enough for two tracks, but only a single track was needed, an earth embankment was provided on top of the bridge, thus easing the gradient. At some time in its history the bridge has been altered and the bricks which were removed became strengthening material for the top of the embankment. The rebuilding undertaken at that time has left the two sides of the bridge displaying, in places, different styles and materials.

From the bridge, the line climbed at 1 in 37 for ¼ mile to Roundwood. When the original line reached this summit the entire area was agricultural, but early in the 1900s houses were built and eventually there was sufficient demand for a halt to be constructed. This comprised a prefabricated platform, approached by a short flight of wooden steps and a small wooden shelter was provided for passengers. Roundwood Halt was opened on 8th August, 1927 and the shelter survived until 1956, when it was sold and removed to a local resident's garden. A footbridge spanned the line above the eastern end of the platform.

Half a mile of straight track took the line over the ridge, then it cut through open countryside, land on the eastern side being owned by Rothamsted Estate. Descending at 1 in 39, through Knott Wood, the gradient then eased off to cross the road from Harpenden to Redbourn via a low plate girder bridge - the strength of which was tested more by the lorries which ran into it, than the trains which ran over it!

Redbourn station, on the down side (east) stood at the foot of the descent. Its buildings were of wood, with the usual offices, but in the end room was a handpump, used to fill a tank in the roof to supply well water to the toilets (about 100 strokes were needed to fill the tank). The toilets drained into a

An aerial view of the National Children's Home and Orphanage at Harpenden *c.* 1930 which also shows the main line (*top right*), the Hemel Hempstead branch on the right, and the route of the former connection to Luton through the cutting curving left.   *Author's Collection*

Ambrose Lane bridge in 1944, the course of the original route to Luton went straight on.
D. Barrie

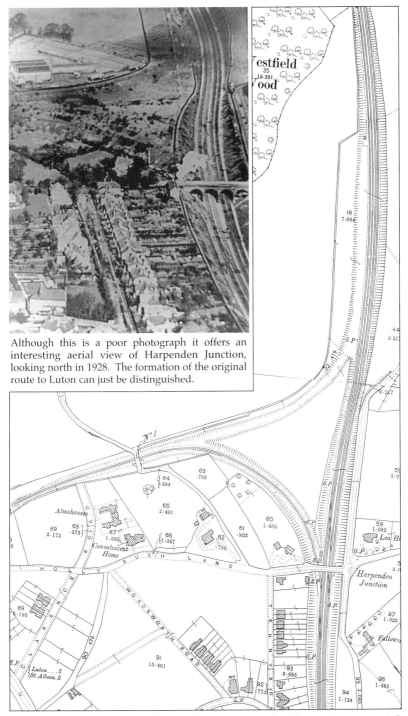

Although this is a poor photograph it offers an interesting aerial view of Harpenden Junction, looking north in 1928. The formation of the original route to Luton can just be distinguished.

Harpenden Junction, showing the branch swinging to the left, the formation of the original route can be clearly seen.   *Reproduced from the 25", 1898 Ordnance Survey Map*

A picture postcard view of Luton Road, Harpenden *c.* 1909. The bridge was known locally as 'The Arch'.

Roundwood Halt in 1946, looking towards Redbourn. *Authors' Collection*

cesspit in the approach road from the Watling Street, where access was covered by a large stone slab. On 22nd January, 1914 work was completed on raising Redbourn's platform to 2 ft 6 in. above rail level, at which time it was surfaced with asphalt and edged with Hamblets' blue coping bricks. This platform was backed by Midland Railway slatted fencing and was lit by gas lamps, with 'Redbourn' on the lamp glasses. A gas lamp also lit the approach road.

A large nameboard with iron letters on a wooden background stood above the fence, but was replaced about 1938 by two LMS totem plates, positioned in a V-shape at the north end of the platform. This type of plate became known as a 'Hawkseye' sign, after its manufacturer, G.C. Hawks of Birmingham. The letters were black, against a background coated with ¾ million minute yellow glass spheres, to give legibility in artificial light as well as daylight.

A whitewashed brick platelayers' hut stood at the up end of the platform, near the ground frame controlling the siding points. At the time of opening Redbourn goods yard was very small, but when the south curve was dug at Harpenden Junction the soil was brought to Redbourn to extend the yard. This gave more coal storage space and enabled the coal siding to be lengthened as far as the Watling Street. A wooden goods shed was positioned over one of the sidings, which for many years was home for a large white owl. Various coal merchants worked from the yard (including Lockharts and Brentnall & Cleland), with office accommodation next to the weighbridge and its hut. The weighbridge had 'Midland Railway' cast into it, and was surrounded by a cobbled area. The goods yard was served by a separate road from that to the station. Well back from the railway, and behind this road, stood the 28 mile post (measured from London). On leaving the station, the line crossed over Watling Street (A5) by means of a plate girder bridge.

Almost immediately the River Ver was crossed by a brick arch bridge, and the railway continued on an embankment through meadow land, only interrupted by a farm track called Connor's Crossing. It was here that the line's builders extracted gravel, carried via a siding which was removed when the line opened. A little further on Chequers Lane was crossed on the skew by another plate girder bridge.

The only public road crossed on the level was at Church End, which led to Flowers Farm, where a crossing keeper's house stood beside the gates. Immediately past the crossing stood Beaumont's Halt, a later addition to the line, being built of sleepers with a cinder surface. The Halt and level crossing were lit by oil lamps, which were tended by a porter from Redbourn, whose job it was to fill, clean and light them. They were extinguished by the guard of the day's last train. The LMS put up one 'Hawkseye' nameplate which remained *in situ* until about 1960 and this is now preserved.

Near Beaumont's Halt, by the 29 milepost, the M1 Motorway (opened in 1959) passed over the line by a concrete bridge, built wide enough to take two tracks. Continuing through undisturbed countryside, a number of farm tracks crossed the line. Once under the double brick arches of Wood End Lane bridge, the gradient stiffened to 1 in 42, easing to 1 in 56 before Claydale Sidings at Three Cherry Trees Lane, where it levelled for a short distance. These sidings served the adjacent brickworks. The gradient then increased to 1 in 39 to reach

Redbourn station *c.* 1920.   *Author's Collection*

Redbourn station in 1959.   *Photomatic*

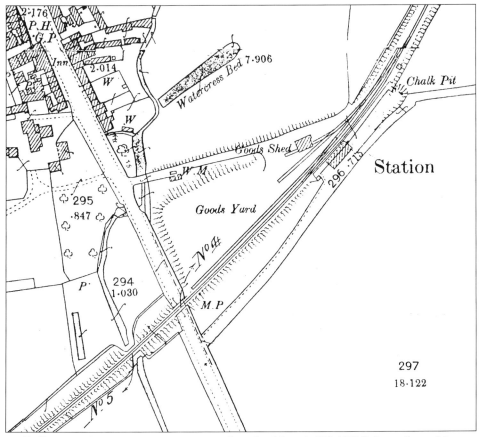

Redbourn station.   *Reproduced from the 25", 1898 Ordnance Survey Map*

Below, left: Redbourn coal yard office, August 1952.   R.E. Lacy

Below, right: Redbourn weighbridge shed, August 1952.   R.E. Lacy

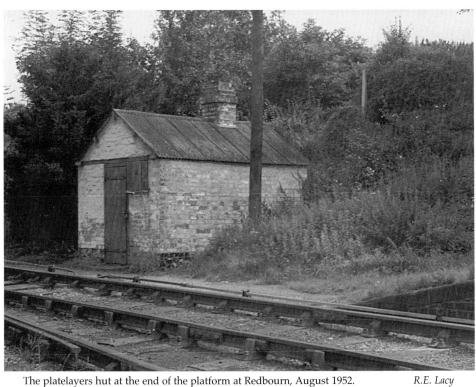

The platelayers hut at the end of the platform at Redbourn, August 1952. *R.E. Lacy*

Bridge No. 6, Chequers Lane bridge near Redbourn, August 1952. *R.E. Lacy*

A Midland Railway 4-4-0 No. 559 is seen on a special train at Beaumont's Halt in 1931. Note the crossing gates appear to be damaged. *John Wood*

Beaumont's Halt still retains its nameboard nine years after passenger services ceased, 21st April, 1956. *S. Summerson*

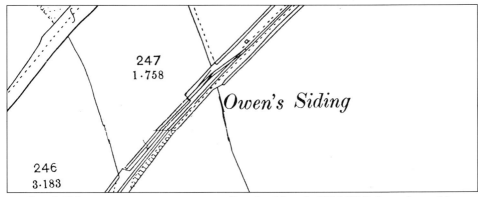

Owen's Siding.

Claydales Brickworks.

Reproduced from the 25″, 1898 Ordnance Survey Map

Reproduced from the 25″, 1925 Ordnance Survey Map

Godwin's Halt.

Reproduced from the 25″, 1925 Ordnance Survey Map

An aerial view of the Hemelite Brick Company's works and Claydale sidings *c.* 1965. The Brocks Fireworks factory is just out of view (*extreme top left*). *Ken Allan*

An aerial view of Godwin's Sidings, Cupid Green *c.* 1950. *Authors' Collection*

Godwin's Halt looking east towards Harpenden *c.* 1950. *D. Gerred*

Johnson '3F' 0-6-0 No. 43245 approaches Godwin's Halt with the Locomotive Club of Great Britain's special train on 11th May, 1957. *A. Willmott*

the line's summit at Cupid Green. It was here that sidings served Mr Godwin's estate, and when a landslip occurred here on 4th June, 1878 the Midland ordered Mr Gratton to purchase another 25 perches of land so that the matter could be resolved. From this summit the descent was at 1 in 39 right down to the platform end of Hemel Hempstead station, and at the top a warning notice instructed drivers of all down goods trains to stop and pin down the wagon brakes before descending.

Just over the summit, still in the cutting, was another later addition - Godwin's Halt - again cheaply constructed using old sleepers for the face and a cinder surface. It was lit by oil lamps and in October 1907 a shelter with a pagoda roof was erected, on trial from its makers (being only the second of its kind on a railway), which was constructed of a material 'like corrugated iron'.

The nearest road to Godwin's Halt was the one to Leverstock Green, which crossed the line by a brick arch, so to reach the Halt passengers had to use field footpaths, although two direction signs were put up. One of the footpaths to Highfield Park crossed the cutting by a wooden footbridge, which by 1928 had become so rickety it was replaced by one with an iron deck. Moving on in time, as the new town of Hemel Hempstead grew new roads came, and Jupiter Drive crossed the line by means of a reinforced concrete bridge, built in 1961 at a cost of £20,000. There was much local anguish because the fencing stopped short of the bridge parapet, and eventually the gap was filled.

Once out of the cutting, the line descended, on a high embankment, crossing Highfield Lane (now Queensway) by a tall brick arch bridge, the retaining walls of which all sported strengthening buttresses. A footpath subway on each side of this bridge was constructed in 1958. Work started on 12th January, when engine No. 43119 arrived with a six-wheeled crane and girders to support the track during the work. A special train of cranes, ballast wagons and wagons of ash, hauled by No. 43873, arrived at 8 am on Sunday, 14th September to remove the girders and make up the track base again.

Adeyfield Road bridge crossed the line by two brick arches at the foot of the incline, and immediately beyond was Hemel Hempstead station, built on the west side of the track. The station site was cut into the hillside and bordered by Midland Road and Crescent Road, giving a triangular site. There was a passing loop through the station, with the goods yard beyond, and extending back behind the station buildings. These buildings were of wood, under a slate roof, and in front was an approach road. On 22nd June, 1882 the Midland Railway Company was asked by Mr Cranstone to contribute towards the repair of the approach road and then to dedicate it to public use, even though the company had, on 14th February, decided to make its own improvements.

Work to raise the station platform to a height of 2 ft 6 in. was completed on 13th February, 1914, and this was backed by the usual slatted fencing (covered with rambling roses). The Midland used a blue and white enamel nameplate, spelling the name 'Hemel Hempsted', but the LMS, replaced this with its 'Hawkseye' nameplates and spelt it with the 'a' included.

In November 1876 John Grover had approached the local gas company with regard to supplying gas at Hemel Hempstead station, but the matter had been deferred until July 1877. The gas company had quoted for gas at 5s. 5d. per

A picture postcard view of Highfield Lane bridge (later known as Queensway bridge).

K. Whiteley

Hemel Hempstead station *c.* 1914.

Authors' Collection

Hemel Hempstead station in 1944.   *D. Gerred*

Hemel Hempstead station *c.* 1925.   *Author's Collection*

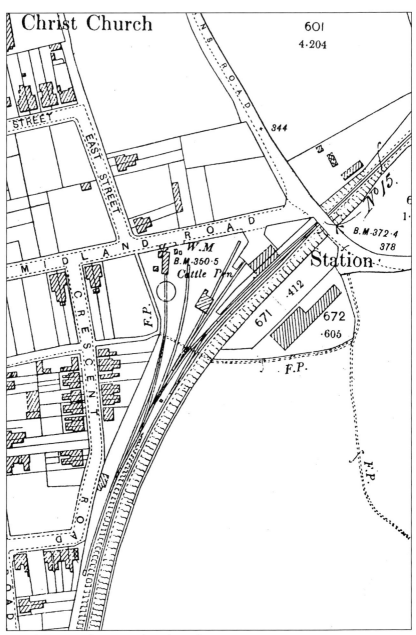

Hemel Hempstead station and goods yard.

Reproduced from the 25", 1898 Ordnance Survey Map

Two views of Hemel Hempstead station in May 1957. *Above*: Looking towards Harpenden, note the steep gradient (1 in 39) beyond the bridge. *Below*: looking towards Heath Park.

(Both) A. Willmott

1,000 feet, plus £50 towards the cost of some 600 yards of gas main pipe. An estimate for installing lights in the engine shed and station came to £47 17s. 3d. The Midland company decided on 3rd July (just prior to opening) that unless the £50 was dropped, and gas supplied at 5s. per 1,000 feet, it would light its premises with oil lights - and it did - until 1894 when gas lamps were erected, lit for the first time on 21st November (ironically, with gas priced at 5s. per 1,000 feet!).

Beside Midland Road stood the wooden engine shed and coal stage, together with a 5 ton crane and the site of the turntable. A goods shed and cattle dock stood behind the station and at the furthest end of the yard, beside Crescent Road, was a stable for railway horses. Near the end of the platform, by the 32½ milepost, a footpath crossed the line and passed through the goods yard. As with other places where footpaths crossed the line, steps were provided down the banks. This particular path had a stile at each end and a flight of steps on the top side only, known locally as the '48 steps', even though there were not that many.

There were many complaints about wagons blocking this path, and as early as March 1879 the Highways Committee were talking of 'compelling the Midland Railway to construct a footbridge over the line'. Exactly one year later the Committee minuted that the company had constructed a level crossing instead and 'should any obstruction occur, persons are requested to inform the station master'. On 29th March, 1881 it was reported that the Midland Railway had kept the crossing clear for the past year. In August 1960 H.E. Webster of Harpenden carried out work to reinstate 50 per cent of the steps, fix the handrail and repair one of the stiles.

The remaining section of line between Hemel Hempstead and Boxmoor stations lay derelict for several years after building, but in 1880 the Midland Railway Company was enticed to open most of it up, in order to deliver coal to the gasworks at Boxmoor, which was being enlarged. Eventually passengers were carried on this section, as far as Heath Park.

Once past Hemel Hempstead goods yard, which was on level ground, the line descended at 1 in 61 through a long cutting and passed under Hillfield Road by a brick bridge. A footpath ran along the top of the bank, but ownership of this was questioned. The railway company considered it to be on its land and therefore it could stop people from using the path, but in 1882 the Council complained about a gate the railway company had installed on it. Surplus land in this area had been estimated to be worth £700 in August 1882 and in July 1884 some of it was sold, including land beside this path.

The line passed under Albion Hill by a brick arch bridge, in the populated area known as Paradise. After leaving the cutting it ran onto an embankment and crossed Marlowes and the River Gade by a substantial three-arch brick viaduct. The embankment gradually lowered as it passed over Boxmoor to Heath Park, an area laid out with grass and flower beds in 1920. The track, as it turned one way and then the other, had a check rail and a 10 mph speed restriction. Hemel Hempstead residents now know this area as the site of the 'Magic Roundabout' - a complex system of mini traffic roundabouts.

Heath Park Halt was opened at the same time as Beaumont's and Godwin's

Marlowes viaduct, Hemel Hempstead *c.* 1950.   *A.D. Edwards*

Marlowes viaduct Hemel Hempstead, 6th July, 1958.   *B. Leslie*

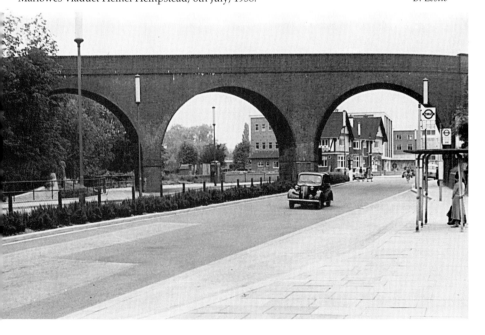

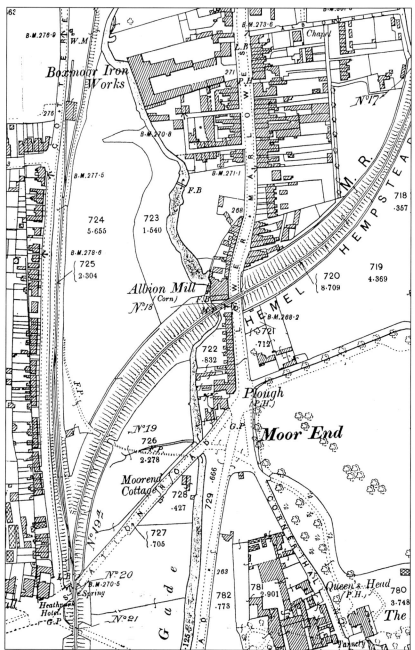

Heath Park and Cotterells Sidings. Heath Park Halt was not opened until 1905, it was sited immediately south of the bridge crossing Station Road.

Reproduced from the 25", 1898 Ordnance Survey Map

Heath Park Halt in 1907 showing a Midland & Great Northern Railway 4-4-0T with a Pullman car. *Lens of Sutton*

An aerial view looking towards Hemel Hempstead *c.* 1935, showing Heath Park Halt (*bottom left*), Cotterells Siding (*left*) and Marlowes viaduct (*top, centre*). *Authors' Collection*

Heath Park Halt looking towards Hemel Hempstead *c.* 1946.   The main line to Hemel Hempstead veers to the right, while the line to Cotterells Siding veers to the left.

Authors' Collection

A view of Heath Park Halt from the road, 6th July, 1958.   *Brian W. Leslie*

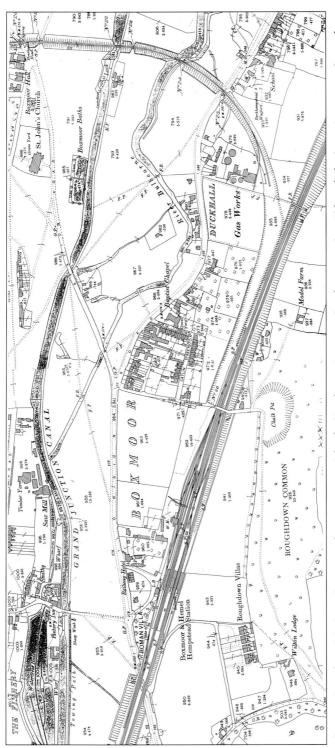

The site of Heath Park Halt can be seen in the extreme top right, the line then swings round to the gas works. Although the formation was made up, there was no physical connection with the LNWR main line at Boxmoor. This connection was not made until 1959 when the line beyond Hemel Hempstead was closed, traffic to the gas works was then served from the Boxmoor end of the line. It was to have only a short life - the gas works closed on 1st April, 1960.

Reproduced from the 25", 1898 Ordnance Survey Map

Boxmoor from Roughdown Road Bridge showing the route of the Harpenden branch on the left through the trees to the gas works, 5th May, 1956. *S. Summerson*

An earlier view from Roughdown Road bridge looking towards Boxmoor goods yard and station, 16th August, 1936. *Adrian Vaughan Collection*

Halts, constructed of timber and built on the west side of the line between two girder bridges. The platform measured 100 ft in length was 9 ft wide and 2 ft 6 in. high, and was approached from road level by a very impressive flight of steps. Backed by the usual slatted fence, there was one nameplate of LMS 'Hawkseye' origin which survived *in situ* until about 1960.

The bridge immediately after the Halt, over Corner Hall Road, was originally planned as a cattle arch but the Highways Committee, in February 1866, demanded no deviation to the road and a proper bridge. The railway company refused, unless compelled. The two sides held a meeting and Mr Balderson reported that the railway company would construct a 20 ft x 12 ft high girder bridge, if the Parish paid the difference in cost, i.e. £179. (Grover had estimated the cost of a cattle arch at £25 and a bridge at £204.) Mr Stallon was adamant that no Parish money should be expended but a close vote (6 for, 5 against) resulted in the bridge being built.

From Heath Park the line was carried on an embankment across the Moor, and when in October 1890 the Boxmoor Trust put seats on the boundary fence, Midland objections forced their removal. The line then crossed the Grand Junction (later Grand Union) Canal at right angles by a plate girder bridge and a similar bridge straddled the River Bulbourne and a farm track. Yet another girder bridge took the line over London Road (A41), from where it immediately curved round towards Boxmoor station. On the inside of this curve was the gasworks, served by its siding. A public footpath ran through the works and across the siding, but a footbridge (planned on 25th November, 1916) was erected for the safety of the path users. A sleeper crossing carried the path over the remains of the branch and a flight of steps was provided up the opposite embankment. The cutting here was very wide, probably due to earth having been removed by the original contractors to provide embankments.

Climbing at 1 in 100, the LNW main line level was reached at Roughdown Road bridge, with its separate arch for the branch, but a Midland Railway trespass notice on the Hemel Hempstead side of the bridge made it clear this was the extent of its ownership. In 1897 the LNWR removed the turntable in its goods yard, which had given the connection to the branch.

A further short section of line was later laid, in the form of sidings with a passing loop, between Heath Park and Cotterells Road and this is dealt with later, in the Goods Traffic chapter.

Bridge Alterations

By the early 1890s there was concern over the condition of some of the original bridges, so a programme of alterations and replacements was started by Mr Hawksworth, the Midland Railway Engineer and superintendent for the London and Bedford area. Plans have come to light which give details of some of these measures and a list is produced below. In order to give as full a picture as possible, bridge alterations carried out at other times have also been included. The bridge numbers given are those allocated by the Midland Railway Company.

A view of Roundwood Halt looking towards Harpenden on 3rd August, 1958, showing the tubular steel footbridge installed in 1951 by Messrs Jarvis.   *Brian W. Leslie*

A 1961 view of Bridge No. 22 over the Grand Union Canal.   *Author's Collection*

No. 2A - Roundwood Footbridge, Harpenden

This was not a railway structure, but was provided by local builders, Messrs Catton, in 1926 for the convenience of those living in the firm's Roundwood and Moreton End developments. Mr Catton was responsible for all maintenance, although the LMS reserved the right to remove it. Built as a wooden trestle structure, it was no doubt beginning to show a need for some expenditure when, in the mid-1940s, he requested Harpenden Urban District Council to take it over, or he would remove it.

In June 1947 agreement was reached between the LMS and Harpenden UDC for it to be taken over as a public footbridge, on payment of £5, on the understanding that the Council would be responsible for any alteration or lengthening if a second track was installed (and this a few weeks before the passenger service was withdrawn!). The Council, however, could also remove it at any time.

By 1951 it needed to be replaced and Messrs Jarvis, another local firm, installed a tubular construction, by Tubewrights of Monmouth, in the week ended 26th September, using two vertical tower cranes to remove the old structure and lift in the new one. In October 1952 the Council received a bill for £51 from British Railways for providing a flagman, to warn of the two or three trains a day which used the branch, while rebuilding was in progress. Councillors were upset by the amount and the delay in sending the bill, for which BR could offer no explanations. However, they did explain that telephone wires had also had to be disconnected to allow the work to proceed, but eventually the Council paid only £20 15s. 3d.

No. 3 Harpenden Lane, Redbourn

This bridge was redecked in 1895, being the first of Hawksworth's replacements.

No. 4 A5 Bridge, Redbourn

Plans for work on this bridge were drawn on 27th August, 1894 and a new deck was installed on 1st July, 1895.

Open-topped buses, it is said, could pass beneath this bridge so long as the conductor requested passengers to duck their heads! To provide adequate headroom, about 1930, the road was lowered, as a safety measure and to stop vehicles from getting jammed under the bridge. However, with the introduction of larger vehicles it became necessary to provide even more headroom, and this was done in 1951, by raising the deck 2 ft and inserting concrete plinths on top of the abutments.

No. 5 River Ver Bridge, Redbourn

Because of its close proximity to Bridge No. 4, similar height adjustments had to be made to this bridge at the same time (1951), although as this was a brick arch the method was different. The track was removed, all the brickwork was raised, including the wing walls, and a float of concrete was laid to raise the level by some 2 ft, on which the track was relaid. The small section of permanent way between these two bridges was then levelled with the bridge works and on either side the track was inclined for a short distance to meet the new level. This resulted in a noticeable hump in the railway.

No. 6 Chequers Lane, Redbourn

A new deck was installed here in 1895, using plans which had been prepared on 17th October, 1894. It still bore the maker's plate in 1965, which showed John Butler & Co., Stanningley, Leeds as Engineers and the Consett Iron & Steel Co., Ltd, as the makers.

No. 10 Cupid Green

In February 1935 an 8 in. gas main was carried over the railway by means of constructing steel support pillars beside the brick arch of this bridge.

No. 15 Adeyfield Road (St Albans Road)

In the early 1930s work started on this bridge, which was immediately at the end of Hemel Hempstead station platform. The purpose was to ease the corner into Midland Road and was done by building a reinforced concrete deck over the platform and adjacent embankment.

No. 16 Infirmary Lane, Hemel Hempstead

A 4 in. gas main and other services were laid over this bridge in June 1912, at which time it was widened.

No. 18 Marlowes Viaduct, Hemel Hempstead

This was a brick construction with the pillars filled with chalk and rubble. Rain water penetrated the trackbed and caused chalky water to seep through the brickwork, discolouring it. In July 1916 the track was lifted and a new asphalt bed was laid, curved to the centre to form a drainage channel, from where water ran with the gradient to the west end of the viaduct, into a drain and eventually into the River Gade running below the third arch.

In 1957 Marlowes was made into a dual carriageway, the middle arch of the viaduct taking the new carriageway. A walkway was built partly over the river, under the third arch.

No. 19 Moor End

A footpath crossed the Moor from Corner Hall to Cotterells Road, over which the railway was originally carried on a small timber bridge. On 13th December, 1887 work started on a brick arch replacement bridge, which was completed on 4th February, 1888.

No. 20 Station Road, Heath Park

Plans for this bridge were drawn on 31st July, 1897, but the rebuilding was not completed until 20th July, 1909. The existing girders were moved out sideways and two girders, which at one time were part of the A41 bridge (No. 25) were used to support the rails.

Station Road was 36 ft wide and the bridge deck weighed 18 tons, but it was 'completely removed' in 1945 when hit by a lorry. The track had to be laid on temporary timber joists while the deck was prepared for lifting back into place.

No. 21 Corner Hall Road, Heath Park

This smaller bridge, at the furthest end of Heath Park Halt platform, was also rebuilt. It weighed 11 tons 16 cwt and this (and Bridge No. 20) were fitted with corrugated iron sides, unlike any others on the line.

No. 22 Canal Bridge

Plans for rebuilding the bridge over the Grand Junction (Union) Canal were prepared in September 1894 but it was not until February 1896 that two new girders were ordered. These were placed under the rails and two girders recovered from Chequers Lane Bridge, Redbourn (No. 6) were placed on the outside, and the deck laid in.

No. 24 River Bulbourne and a Farm Track

Plans for this bridge were drawn on 18th August, 1897 and rebuilding involved placing two 38 ft 6 in. girders under the rails. The cross planks forming the deck were 16 ft wide, and handrails were fitted at the edge. In 1931 the bridge was strengthened by inserting a substantial timber prop in the centre.

No. 25 A41 - London Road Bridge

This 41 ft span bridge was also strengthened in 1931 when two girders, recovered from the Canal Bridge (No. 22), which had been in store, were used to replace the two outer girders. This bridge also carried a gas main.

A view of London Road bridge on 18th April, 1964, shortly before its demolition.

R.M. Casserley

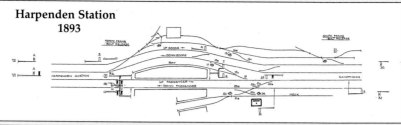

Harpenden Station 1893

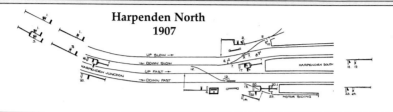

Harpenden North 1907

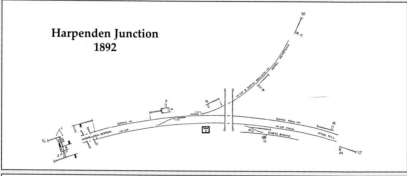

Harpenden Junction 1892

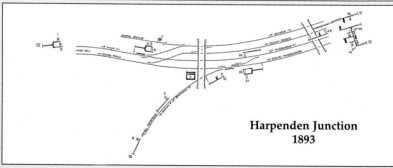

Harpenden Junction 1893

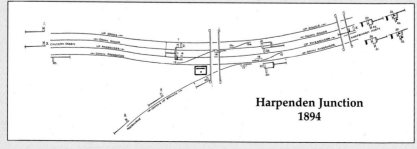

Harpenden Junction 1894

Chapter Seven

Signalling

When the Hemel Hempstead line was built the Midland Railway main line to London had only two tracks. A signal box was built at the junction with the branch in 1876, on the up side of the main line, with entry from the branch being protected by a home and a distant signal. It was this signal box which suffered fire damage in February 1877, and on 3rd April instructions were given for its rebuilding, with the cost to come from the Fire Insurance Fund. Once open, communication with Hemel Hempstead was made by telegraph instruments, but this was soon considered unsatisfactory and the Midland's Way & Works Committee agreed on 16th October, 1877 to provide speaking telegraph instruments at a cost of £28 10s. This move enabled the company to dispense with the junior clerk then employed to work the telegraph at the junction.

When the south facing junction was opened in 1888, this signal box was demolished and the points were finally removed on 6th January, 1890. The new junction was worked from a temporary signal box with 12 levers, again on the up side of the main line, opposite the branch points. On 13th March, 1892 a new signal box was opened, built in the fork of the branch and the main lines, just north of Hollybush Lane bridge. It contained 32 levers, in readiness for the opening of the goods lines through Harpenden (making the main line quadruple track).

At this time a home signal was erected between Hollybush Lane bridge and the branch connection to the main line, but it was so poorly sighted, being hidden by the bridge, that an outer home signal was provided near Ambrose Lane bridge, with a distant signal beyond that. When the 1892 signal box opened these signals remained, but only two years later a new 32 lever frame was fitted in the signal box, and at the same time an outer distant signal was provided - 1,007 yards along the branch, well past Roundwood summit. In view of the route the operating wire had to take, it is doubtful whether anyone managed to work it, and it was removed just a few months later. The inner home signal protecting the main line was moved back to a slightly better position in front of the bridge, but still on the 'wrong' side of the line.

In May 1905 a spark from an engine ignited the platform on the down home bracket signal and a lamp lad working nearby summoned help from Harpenden station. The station master arrived on a light engine and water was carried up the ladder to douse the flames. The signal stayed in use until it was replaced by the LMS in 1935. The new one comprised upper quadrant arms on pitch pine posts, with flat finials. Between the signal and the branch a set of trailing points connected the up and down main lines for the use of branch trains.

The distant signal (near Roundwood Halt) was replaced in 1928, when the LMS installed one of its experimental round concrete posts, fitted with an upper quadrant arm, fixed at caution. A fogman's hut was also provided.

The outer and inner home signals were renewed in 1947 with upper quadrant signals on tubular posts, at which time the inner home was moved to a much better

Signalman J. Woodward can be seen in this 1938 view of Harpenden Junction signal box.
Authors' Collection

Harpenden Junction signal box as seen from the Hemel Hempstead branch in 1946.   *D. Barrie*

position on the curve, well before the signal box. A fireman's call plunger was also installed by the outer home signal to warn signalmen of the arrival of a train.

Turning now to Redbourn, from 1877 there was a home and distant signal in each direction, but these were removed in 1887. The points into the sidings were controlled by Midland economical point levers, i.e. the point rodding was connected to a slide bar with a slot along it, which, when moved, the first part unlocked the point, the middle section (being angled) moved the point and the last straight part of the slot relocked the point. One lever, therefore, did the work of two. Also in the point rodding was an Annett's Key lock which could only be released with the staff inserted; the staff only being released when the points were restored to their correct position. The points in the yard were worked by weighted hand levers.

Beside Beaumont's Halt was the only public road to cross the line on the level and initially two flagmen were employed to protect it. Disregarding its earlier Agreement with the Hemel company, in August 1879 the Midland decided to provide a gatehouse, gates and a distant signal in each direction, worked from a two-lever frame between the house and the track. In December W. Vigar's estimate of £332 0s. 6d. was accepted, being the lowest of three tenders submitted for the house, but his final bill amounted to £311 10s. 10d. The signals cost £80 and the gates £30.

Mrs Emily Thompson, wife of a platelayer, was the first gatekeeper and started work on 5th July, 1880. The two flagmen were dispensed with at a saving of £83 4s. per annum. About 50 yards from the gates, a signal lamp was mounted on a short post to show a white light at night, as a marker for the crossing. The distant signals were replaced in August 1947 with upper quadrant signals on tubular posts and the lever frame was overhauled at the same time. For some years, while a gatekeeper lived in the house, the signals were worked but these were later fixed at caution and the train crews had to open and shut the gates.

The brickworks at Claydale had a shunting loop siding and the points at each end were controlled by a single lever and staff box. At Godwin's Sidings, initially, a signal box, situated on the down side of the line, controlled the points, plus a home and distant signal in each direction. The signals and signal box were removed early on and replaced by a single lever for the main point into the sidings.

Hemel Hempstead commenced with distant, home and starting signals in each direction but these were removed on 6th April, 1887. The points at Adeyfield Road bridge had a lever fixed beside them, while the points at the other end were worked from a three-lever frame. The points into the sidings at Cotterells and the gasworks were controlled by economical point locks worked by a single lever, some bearing 1892 castings.

All the points at the stations and sidings were last renewed between 1947 and 1950, and on 24th November, 1957 a new Harpenden Junction signal box came into use, which had been built alongside its 60 year old predecessor. This signal box was to a standard BR design, with 45 levers. Here the train crew picked up the single line staff (with Annett's Key), the branch being worked on a 'one engine in steam' basis. Some firemen, when getting ready to return the staff to the signalman would 'accidentally' heat it up by holding the signalman's end near the firebox door, thus resulting in some lively handovers! The spare train

The 1957-built Harpenden Junction signal box seen on 3rd August, 1958.

B. Leslie

The up distant signal at Beaumont's Halt crossing in 1957.

A. Willmott

staff had to be requisitioned from Bedford signal stores in about 1955, after the original was snapped in two when a large lump of coal landed on it.

At the junction a catch point was installed by the branch inner home signal on 5th December, 1965. A detonator placer had been installed here in 1957 but was adapted on 1st May, 1966 when its rodding was connected to the catch point instead. At the same time the inner and outer home signals were removed and a disc shunting signal was installed by the new point. Even at this date it was fitted with an LMS repeater contact box. The approach to the signal was track-circuited for the first time, and in January 1965 an AWS ramp was fitted on the approach to the fixed distant signal at Roundwood, but it was removed in 1977.

Problems arose in this area in the latter days of BR working, when children often tampered with the fireman's call plunger, leaving the signalman in doubt as to the arrival of a train. To overcome this train crews would telephone the signalman from Redbourn, giving an expected arrival time at the junction, but this was sometimes thwarted by the theft of telephone wires. The only solution was for the train to stop at the signal, whistle loudly and hope to be heard. If the signal went up the driver would proceed, but if not, the fireman had to walk from Ambrose Lane bridge to the junction to inform the signalman of their presence. To avoid this walk trains sometimes crept round the corner against the signal.

When the Hemelite Company took over the line in 1968, two limit of shunt lamps were installed by Ambrose Lane bridge and the down home signal onto the branch was removed, although the post remained until it was replaced in 1977 by a straight post signal, as there were then no facing movements onto the branch. Access was from the up fast line, protected by disc shunting signals.

On 29th April, 1968 BR signal engineers removed the train staff locks from the points at Claydale and Redbourn and replaced them with two-way reversible levers so that any point could be moved. The old levers and locks remained in the undergrowth for many years.

The 'One Engine in Steam' staff (*back and front*) for the Hemel Hempstead branch.

On **MONDAY, JULY 16th, 1877**, and until further notice, the Branch Line will be opened for **PASSENGER and GOODS Traffic**, and Trains will run on **Weekdays** as under :—

STATIONS.	1 Passenger	2 Passenger	3 Passenger	4 Passenger	5 Goods, &c.	6
	a. m.	p. m.	p. m.	p. m.	p. m.	
LUTON ....dep.	9 45	12 40	3 45	6 40	8 40	..
Chiltern Green .... { arr.					8 ..	..
Harpenden Junction .... { dep.	9 55	12 50	3 55	6 50	8 55	..
	9*59	12*54	3*59	6*54	8*55	..
Redbourn .... { arr.	..	..	..	..	9 7	..
{ dep.	10 9	1 4	4 9	7 4	9 12	..
Goodwin's Siding	..	..	..	..		..
HEMEL HEMPSTEAD.... ....arr.	10 25	1 20	4 25	7 20	9 30	..

Miles	STATIONS.	7 Passenger	8 Passenger	9 Passenger	10 Passenger	11 Goods, &c.	12
		a. m.	a. m.	p. m.	p. m.	p. m.	
..	HEMEL HEMPSTEAD ....dep.	7 55	11 10	2 20	5 45	7 35	..
1¼	Goodwin's Siding..................	..	..	..	..		..
4¼	Redbourn .... { arr.					7 60	..
	{ dep.	8 8	11 23	2 33	5 58	7 55	..
7¼	Harpenden Junction	8*23	11*38	2*48	6*10	8*10	..
9	Chiltern Green .... { arr.						..
	{ dep.	8 27	11 42	2 52	6 14		..
11	LUTON........................arr.	8 35	11 50	3 0	6 22	8 25	

The Branch is a **Single Line**, and will be worked by **Staff only**, the Staff Stations being **Harpenden Junction** and **Hemel Hempstead**.

The first timetable.

The 1903 timetable note the spelling 'Hemel Hempsted'.

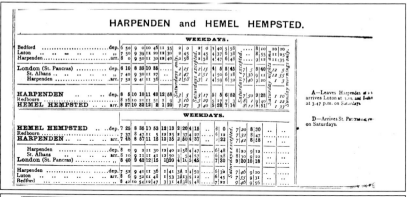

The 1937 timetable.

Chapter Eight

Engines, Trains and Travellers

Just a week after the branch opened, the Oddfellows & Foresters' 7th Annual Fete was held on Monday, 23rd July, in the grounds of The Bury, Hemel Hempstead, by permission of Mr Sansom. The Midland Railway Company consented to issue specially priced tickets for people wishing to attend. 1st and 3rd class return tickets were sold at single rates for double journeys from St Albans, Harpenden, Chiltern Green and Luton, and return fares of 1s. (1st Class) and 6d. (3rd Class) were available from Redbourn. Tickets were only available on the day of travel but passengers were allowed to use any of the timetabled trains to get there, returning on a special train which left Hemel Hempstead at 7.35 pm. (For the record, it was a very wet day and the Fete made a loss of between £20 and £30!)

The first regular timetable showed four passenger trains running each way over the branch, plus an evening goods train, but by November 1877 only three trains were timetabled, leaving Hemel Hempstead at 8.50 am, 11.10 am and 5.40 pm, and returning from Luton at 10 am, 3 pm and 6.45 pm. This service remained until 1888.

One of the first locomotives on the line was Kirtley '50' class 2-4-0 No. 14, which remained in use until about 1880. Three 2-4-0 tanks, built by George England & Co. for the Somerset & Dorset Railway Company in 1863 (numbers 9, 10 and 13) were purchased in August 1878 by the Midland Railway Company and renumbered 1397-9. These came to the branch mid-1881 and stayed for several years. Later they were the only locomotives allowed beyond Hemel Hempstead to the gasworks.

Although originally much importance was put on the benefits of linking Hemel Hempstead with Luton, it soon became clear that many passengers needed to get to London - this was the advent of the commuter age! Hemel Hempstead travellers were irritated by having to journey across country and then wait at Chiltern Green or Luton to get to London, and some had moved over to the LNWR route, using the latter's horse bus (*see Chapter Nine*) to take them to Boxmoor station.

So strong was the feeling that in February 1887 a public meeting was held at Hemel Hempstead Town Hall, attended also by Redbourn residents, to consider the desirability of requesting the Midland Railway Company to improve the service of trains 'with a view to rendering communications between Hemel Hempstead and London more direct and expeditious'. One gentleman complained that after a two hour journey he thought he must be in London, only to find the train was pulling into St Albans. Another remarked there was a 'better service of trains in the backwoods of America' and a businessman said 'it took half a day to get to London, and half a day back, leaving no time to transact business'. It was therefore resolved to ask the Midland Railway Company to 'complete the line to Harpenden as originally projected', suggesting it would be very remunerative to the company.

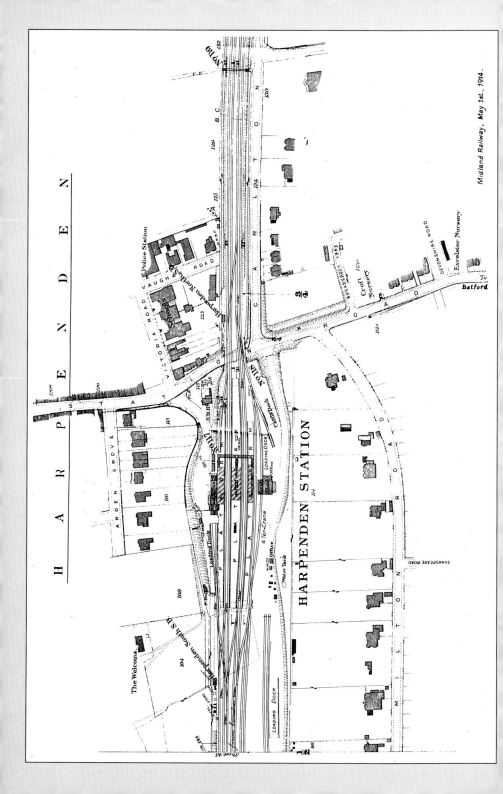

Midland Railway, May 1st., 1914.

The meeting appointed a deputation comprising the High Bailiff, (Mr M. Leno), Mr Lovel Smeathman (a solicitor), Revd Dr Robbins and Mr Cranstone, and applied for an audience with the Midland Directors. The Midland Board agreed to this request on 18th February and were sufficiently swayed by their arguments that the problem was immediately put in the hands of the Traffic Committee, who came up with a plan to abandon the Luton-facing junction at Harpenden, replacing it with an 11-chain radius curve 'in the direction of London', which they thought could be built for about £6,500.

On 19th May Mr Gratton was authorised to buy the necessary land 'for a sum not exceeding £300' and he reported on 14th July that this had been done at a cost of £250. Plans and estimate submitted by the Traffic Committee were 'read' by the Board on 11th August and 15th September, and on 21st October, 1887 Mr Underwood and Mr Gratton were 'desired to prepare the necessary plans and sections for deposit for the South Curve under the Additional Powers Bill'. In fact it was approved by Parliament as 'The Harpenden Curve'.

Work commenced on 1st November, 1887 and Mr Rolt of Harpenden got the contract to supply horses and carts. To avoid purchasing extra land, which would have involved dealing with another landowner, a large retaining wall was built beside the new track. The work was ready for inspection on 4th June, 1888 and on 15th June the BOT Inspector, Major Mandarin, submitted his report. The curve, 18.39 chains in length, had been built with standard Midland type track, being 85 lb. per yard steel rail, and having a check rail throughout. 50 lb. chairs and 100 lb. check rail chairs were held in place by outside keys, and two spikes and two tree nails in each chair. Sleepers were spaced 2 ft 2 in. apart at the point, 2 ft 5 in. next to the point and 2 ft 10 in. elsewhere. The ballast was made up of broken slag, gravel and ashes.

Having been authorised to use the new route, the Midland began running trains over it and into Harpenden station on 2nd July, 1888, at which time the Luton-facing curve was abandoned. To coincide with opening, the passenger service was increased to seven trains a day in each direction. The 3.50 pm from Hemel Hempstead went on to St, Albans, arriving there at 4.28 pm, returning from there at 4.56 pm and arriving back at Hemel Hempstead at 5.35 pm. This train continued to run until October 1893, when the up train was retimed to run 5 minutes later and in July 1894 the down train was retimed to run 3 minutes earlier, but in October 1895 the service was discontinued.

Despite wet and rough weather, some 200 tickets were issued to people wishing to travel over the new route on opening day. Although they considered the direct route advantageous, they were disappointed with the expensive fares. At that time the LNWR was charging 2s. single fare to London, and 3s. 7d. return, whereas the new Midland fares were 2s. 6d. single and 5s. return. It would appear that the 'fares grievance' was still being aired in January 1907 because Redbourn Parish Council recorded in its Minutes that efforts were being made to get fares reduced between Redbourn and St Albans. It was pointed out that, at a fare of 1s. 4d. return, it was cheaper, when two or three persons travelled together, to hire a conveyance rather than travel by train. If fares were causing one problem, then lack of information was causing another, which prompted the following anonymous letter to a local newspaper

A Johnson 'Single' passes through Harpenden with a London-bound train *c.* 1895.

Authors' Collection

A down express at Harpenden station *c.* 1895.   *Authors' Collection*

on 15th September, 1888, just a couple of months after the new curve had come into use:

> Is it quite true that the Midland Railway Company are working the line between Harpenden and Hemel Hempstead? On arrival at the former place from London the other day I saw no notice that there was any junction and only in a very faint voice did I hear a Porter say 'Change here for Hemel Hempstead and Redbourn'. Well, I say this does not sound very businesslike. One would have thought that after laying out some £3/4,000 to improve the line and after putting a lot of trains on, at least the Company would, like all other tradesmen, advertise the affair.

Perhaps the writer also communicated direct with the railway company, as in due course a large noticeboard was erected at Harpenden station advising travellers of the need to change trains for the branch.

However, not every request to the Midland Railway Company was dealt with so positively, as the Revd W.A. Pope found out. He wrote to the Midland Board requesting a subscription from them towards 'the erection of a vicarage house at Redbourn', but the Board 'declined'. In November 1888, though, Mr Gratton (the Midland's Land Agent and Secretary of their Way & Works Committee, who had been involved with the Harpenden Curve) died suddenly, and the Board presented £1,000 to his widow 'in recognition of his services'.

By 1892 Beyer, Peacock 2-4-0s Nos. 197, 199, 232 and 233 were in use regularly on the branch, and on 17th September, 1896 the Midland Locomotive Committee proposed the construction of a water tank at Harpenden to serve the goods tank engines they were intending to introduce. The 1897 Working Timetable Appendix refers to the section beyond Hemel Hempstead, on which no locomotives heavier than these '1380' class standard Johnson 0-6-0Ts were to work, but in July 1905 the larger '2757' class Johnson 0-6-0Ts were introduced.

Right from the beginning there were offers of cheap tickets and excursions to special events near and far. One of the first over the new curve route was on 29th August, 1888, bringing Hemel Hempstead and Redbourn people to Harpenden for the 10th Flower Show. Cheap tickets were also available for supporters to attend Luton Town's football matches, e.g. on 30th, January, 1897 the return fare from Hemel Hempstead was 1s. 3d., provided passengers travelled by the 12 noon or 2.28 pm, trains.

Many 'Cook's Tours' were run and some of these offered country-dwellers the chance of a very long day out at the seaside - starting as early as 5 am and not returning until late in the evening. These trips were advertised at the stations by means of handbills and sometimes large posters. Some appeared as notices in the local press, as did train timetables and other relevant notices, such as the one which appeared on 28th June, 1901, advising the public that the postbox by Redbourn Post Office would be cleared at 8.30 am, instead of 9.10 am, to allow the mail to catch a re-scheduled branch train.

Although the branch was well used for excursions, Hempsteadians still felt let down by the Midland for the poor service they were running for London-bound passengers, particularly their unwillingness to move towards a link at Boxmoor. One should remember that by this time straw plaiting was virtually extinct in the Hemel Hempstead area and the town was growing. Business

Looking down the approach road towards the station master's house at Harpenden *c.* 1935.

Lens of Sutton

A 1930 view from the north end of Harpenden station showing Harpenden North signal box.

Authors' Collection

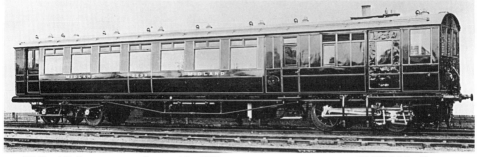

Midland Railway steam railmotor No. 2233.   *BR/OPC Joint Venture*

A view from Adeyfield Road of a steam railmotor at work, 26th March, 1905.   *M. Stanyon*

A steam rail motor is seen at the newly-built Heath Park Halt in 1905.   *Authors' Collection*

...LAND RAILWAY.

AUGMENTED SERVICE

BY

RAIL MOTOR

BETWEEN

HEMEL HEMPSTED
REDBOURN & HARPENDEN

OCTOBER 1st, 1905, to MARCH 31st, 1906
(unless previously cancelled).

There is only one class of carriage on the Branch.

		a.m.	a.m.	a.m.	M a.m.	M p.m.	M p.m.	M p.m.	M p.m.	M p.m.	M p.m.	M p.m.
Heath Park Halt	dep.	7 20	8 32	10 51	12 46	2 20	3 35	5 16	6 32	8 10		
HEMEL HEMPSTED	,,	7 24	8 36	10 58	12 55	2 32	3 39	5 20	6 38	8 14		
Godwin's Halt	,,	7 29	8 41	11 4	12 59	2 37	3 44	5 25	6 44	8 21		
Beaumont's Halt	,,	7 35	8 48	11 12	1 9	2 42	3 49	5 30	6 49	8 31		
Redbourn	,,	7 45	8 57	11 22	1 20	2 52	4 0	5 40	6 54	8 41		
HARPENDEN	arr.	8 40	9 40	12 10	2 27	4 12	4 42	7 5	7 5	9 50		
LONDON (St. Pancras)	arr.											

		a.m.	a.m.	a.m.	M p.m.	M p.m.	M p.m.	M p.m.	M p.m.	M p.m.	M p.m.
LONDON (St. Pancras)	dep.	6 10	9 20	10 35	1 5	2 18	4 0	5 12	6 33	8 40	
HARPENDEN	dep.	7 57	10 15	11 44	1 43	2 58	4 38	5 56	7 18	9 25	
Redbourn		8 8	10 27	11 56	1 56	3 14	4 49	6 11	7 29	9 36	
Beaumont's Halt		8 12	10 31	12 0	2 0	3 18	4 53	6 17	7 33	9 40	
Godwin's Halt		8 19	10 37	12 6	2 6	3 24	4 59	6 21	7 39	9 46	
HEMEL HEMPSTED		8 22	10 41	12 12	2 10	3 28	5 3	6 21	7 43	9 50	
Heath Park Halt	arr.		10 46	12 18	2 16			6 27			

M Rail Motor Coach.

TICKETS. Passengers travelling by the Motor Coaches from the Stations must obtain their tickets at the Station Booking Offices, and must produce them on entering the Coach. Passengers joining the Coaches at the "Halts," will be booked by the Conductor on the Coach. To prevent delay in the working of the Motor Service, Passengers are respectfully requested to tender the exact fare to the Conductor.
Children under three years of age travel free; those above three and under twelve at half price.

PARCELS. Parcels will be conveyed between the Stations only, and not to and from the "Halts."

SMOKING. Passengers are respectfully requested to refrain from Smoking in the Motor Coaches.

LUGGAGE. The Company do not undertake to handle luggage at the "Halts."

Derby, 1905.

JOHN MATHIESON, General Manager.

people were beginning to commute in greater numbers and therefore they wished to travel comfortably and via the most direct service. The people of Hemel Hempstead were faced with an inferior service on the branch, which did not connect with main line trains at Harpenden, or an inconvenient journey to Boxmoor LNWR station. During 1902 and 1903 these criticisms were strongly addressed to the railway companies through newspaper editorials, letters and Committee reports, together with direct communications - with a little success.

In April 1902 Hemel Hempstead Council heard from the Midland declining to run a through train to St Pancras, but putting on an extra train each way in the morning. The Mayor acknowledged that they 'must be thankful for small mercies' and hoped for something better to follow!

'The Man in the Moon', a local newspaper columnist, also campaigned for better things - but he had bigger ideas. In November 1902, instead of the 'out of the way, poky and quite insufficient little station' (Hemel Hempstead), he called for the line to be doubled and a new station built on 'the bridge bank in Marlowes', which would be an 'act of common sense business'. He considered a through service to Boxmoor would be 'one of the easiest feats of engineering to perform, for a single line exists right up to the gasworks'. The following week he even suggested a new station could be built at the end of Cotterells (as if there was not enough clamour already over the goods traffic!).

For a while the Midland had run a late 'Saturday Night' train on the branch, leaving Harpenden at 1.10 am (for travellers on the 12.05 am from London) and at its January 1903 meeting Hemel Hempstead Council considered a request for support from Redbourn Council, that this train should also be run on Wednesdays. The general feeling was in favour, but Councillor Hodgson opposed, saying 'all respectable people should be in bed at midnight'! Following this meeting, the *Hemel Hempstead Gazette* carried out a public survey which showed a need, not for a 'midnight train', but for an evening train, as the then 6.10 pm from Harpenden was too early for London commuters and the 8.40 pm was too late and involved a long wait. The Midland answered this at the end of April by putting on a 7.50 pm train.

More excursions followed and ticket sales almost reached a record for the branch on the Saturday and Monday of 1904 Whitsun Bank Holiday weekend, when over 500 people booked for various places, mainly Harpenden and St Albans, resulting in crowded trains, on one of which sixteen 3rd class passengers travelled in a 1st class compartment. In June 1904 the Midland Railway Company introduced trips from St Pancras and Kentish Town into the country, including Hemel Hempstead and these were well supported.

In 1905 the Midland Railway Company carried out some important changes to the branch - perhaps they had at last listened to their passengers' demands. However, at this time the company was trying to increase passenger revenue, but at the same time rationalise expenditure on motive power. This was the era of the 'Rail-Motor', and the Midland Railway had already introduced two steam railmotors on the Morecambe to Heysham line. On Sunday 26th March, 1905 one of these was brought to Harpenden from Derby, arriving at 10.30 am and it left almost immediately for a trial run on the Hemel Hempstead branch.

In the railmotor coach were Mr G. Arnold (district superintendent of St

Two views of Midland & Great Northern Railway 4-4-0T No. 19 with a Pullman car at Harpenden station in 1906. *(Both) Science Museum*

Pancras), Mr Fowler (a gas engineer), Mr Bagwell (of the Superintendent's Department), Mr Pratt (of the Locomotive Department) and Mr G. Patter (district inspector). On reaching Hemel Hempstead station Mr Cross (the station master) joined the party and the coach carried on as far as the gasworks at Boxmoor, where it remained for a few minutes before returning to Harpenden. Shortly after mid-day another trip was made to Hemel Hempstead and back, this time with a horsebox attached. This being successful, another trip was made later in the afternoon, with a goods van and a horsebox attached. This was considered a severe test and the officials were most satisfied. Whilst speed was not the object, the journey took less than 25 minutes.

Because steam railmotors were 'an engine and coach all-in-one' they did not need large stations, and so it was decided to build some new Halts on the branch, which would open with the introduction of a railmotor service. These were to be at Beaumont's Lane, Redbourn, at Godwin's (just west of the sidings) and at Heath Park on the former goods-only section. A plan exists showing a proposed Halt at Wood End (between Beaumont's and Godwin's) but this idea was obviously abandoned. Indeed, when the local newspaper first heard of these innovations it announced a whole series of locations for halts, starting at Harpenden (a mile from the station) and working right through to a 'terminus' at Roughdown Road bridge - it soon became clear this was just wishful thinking!

The three Halts were hastily planned and quickly constructed during June, with Heath Park Halt platform being completed on the 19th. This was followed, in July, by provision of a water supply to the siding next to the down fast line at Harpenden, where it was intended the railmotor would be stabled overnight. At Hemel Hempstead it was to obtain water from a hydrant on the platform.

During the Board of Trade inspection, on 29th July, 1905, all the new works were observed, but the section between Hemel Hempstead and Heath Park received the most scrutiny because the track was to be used by passenger trains for the first time. The Inspector found this section comprised 24 ft-long rails, which had weighed 85 lb. per yard when originally laid, but which had deteriorated to 79 lb. per yard. Chairs of 40 lb. were each fixed by two iron spikes and two tree nails. The track was inside-keyed, using oak keys. Sleepers were creosoted Baltic timber and the ballast was Bedford gravel.

The Inspector's only adverse comment was that, for a railmotor, the platforms at Hemel Hempstead and Redbourn would be rather low. This was solved by the Midland's promise to provide steps for passengers to use when boarding and leaving the carriage. The new service was seen as similar to a tramway, thus the halts were unmanned and no parcels service operated from them. The branch was almost unique in that its passenger service had a Halt for its terminus (Heath Park).

Having received the Inspector's approval, the new service started on Wednesday, 9th August and was a combination of railmotor and engine-and-coach operation. Because the previously used rolling stock made trains too long to be accommodated at the Halts, the Midland introduced a shorter pairing, being a tank engine with a Pullman coach. This coach had previously been used on the main line and at the time was not fitted for push and pull working (a

A selection of tickets

conversion which was carried out in January 1906). The new timetable indicated three journeys each way for the engine and Pullman coach, two in the morning and one in the evening from Hemel Hempstead and the reverse from Harpenden.

The remaining six journeys each way were undertaken by the railmotor, which was one of those previously mentioned (either No. 2233 or No. 2234), which had been overhauled at Derby ready for service on the branch. When this unusual vehicle was tested its presence aroused much interest both in Harpenden and Hemel Hempstead and, once inside it, passengers would most certainly have noticed a change from their normal trains. The railmotor was 60 feet long, made up of an engine compartment, with coal space, a luggage compartment, a passenger area and an end vestibule, also with driving controls. The vehicle had seating for 54 passengers - but these were mainly pairs of wooden seats, with no upholstery. As one passenger said 'the interior was scarcely as comfortable as the ordinary carriage' but 'there was no bumping, as expected'. The carriage was lit by gas and Midland handbills 'Respectfully requested passengers to refrain from smoking in the Motor Coaches'.

To use the railmotor, passengers joining at stations booked in the normal way, whilst those using the Halts were checked by a conductor taking fares for travel on the branch only. To facilitate longer-distance passengers, and save them crossing the footbridge to the main ticket office, one of the waiting rooms on the up platform at Harpenden was converted into a second ticket office. The service was well patronised and pleas were soon forthcoming for all trains to start from Heath Park (only a few during the day and one evening train originally did this). Hopes of more Halts, or even the long-awaited station at Boxmoor, were raised higher on Wednesday 27th September, 1905 when Mr John Mathieson (Midland General Manager) and other chief officials visited Hemel Hempstead and inspected the line as far as the gasworks. The purpose of the visit was not made public, and no further expansion was undertaken.

Around this time a so-called 'novelty trip' from Hemel Hempstead to Heath Park, costing 1d., was a great attraction for people wanting to spend an afternoon on the Moor, and it was hoped 'the 6.33 pm, from Heath Park would bring a host of people to the town for shopping'! The 12.36 pm from Hemel Hempstead to Heath Park was seen as a great advantage to workmen, who could get home to lunch in five minutes.

When the winter timetable came into effect on 1st October, 1905 a handbill, giving details of the 'Augmented Service by Rail Motor' still showed only certain trains going through to, or starting from, Heath Park. However, some improvements were made insofar as connections with main line trains at Harpenden were concerned. On reflection, it is probably fair to say that at this time the branch was working satisfactorily, and Hemel Hempstead people had welcomed the new service, but it soon encountered a setback.

At 6.38 pm on 24th October, 1905 the railmotor failed, half a mile out of Hemel Hempstead. Harpenden station was quickly telegraphed, but no engine could be dispatched immediately 'to enable the train to be run in accordance with the Company's timetable'. The tank engine and Pullman coach eventually arrived to provide a service to Harpenden, and also to bring back the failed

A fine view of a Midland & Great Northern 4-4-0T with a Pullman car in the bay platform at Harpenden in 1906. *L&GRP*

Hemel Hempstead station, with a Pullman car in the yard *c*. 1910. *Authors' Collection*

HEMEL HEMSTEAD. M

railmotor, but considerable delays occurred and many passengers missed their main line connections. The railmotor, therefore, in spite of its successful trials, and contrary to expectations, did not prove suitable for the branch and was withdrawn from service. The engine and Pullman car then took over the complete service, but because of the popularity of the branch a need arose for increased capacity. This was met, at the end of the year, when a 4-wheeled coach, No. 0666, built in 1878, was converted into a motor trailer, with three 3rd class open compartments. This was originally ordered to run with the railmotor, but it was ultimately used with other stock.

A further change occurred on 2nd April, 1906, when the tank engine and Pullman coach were replaced. Another, though smaller, Pullman coach came in its place, hauled by a Hudswell, Clarke & Rogers 4-4-0T loaned from the Midland & Great Northern Railway, under an agreement whereby four of these engines (Nos. 8, 10, 19 and 40) were exchanged for three 0-4-4 side tank engines Nos. 141-3) for six years. The first one to use the branch was No. 19, still with its oval brass numberplate and the yellow livery of its former owners, the Yarmouth & North Norfolk Railway.

Early in 1906 it was announced that considerable alterations were to be made to accommodate branch trains at Harpenden station, and in May workmen began digging out a new bay platform at the north end of the down fast platform, at which time a water supply was also laid in. The bay, which was long enough to hold an engine and one coach, was completed at the end of June, but did not come into use until the end of July, when the new Harpenden North signal box opened, which controlled it. The bay was only connected to the down main line, so passengers on up branch trains got off at Harpenden's up fast platform, after which the train ran through the station, reversed on to the down fast line and ran back through the station, to enable it to reverse into the bay. Down branch trains started from the bay, unless more coaches were in use. On these occasions passengers boarded on the down fast platform.

Whilst the railway company was busy making improvements, the public were busy attending important local events. Heavy bookings were made for the Great Horse and Dog Show, held in Harpenden in 1906, but events like these created problems for the railway company and, in turn, this drew criticism from travellers, as the following letter demonstrates:

> Having cause to travel on the Midland Railway on Saturday last to Hemel Hempstead, which arrives there about 9.40 (pm), I was subject to considerable annoyance by the conduct of a portion of the passengers who joined the train at Harpenden. The language was shocking in the extreme and was so bad at one time that the ticket examiner had to speak to a man. I consider it disgraceful that on account of it being one carriage in which all the passengers had to herd, that ladies and children were subjected to the distressing annoyance of men using foul words.
>
> Surely on the occasion of such things as race meetings the Railway Company should see, by providing more than one carriage on the trains, that the comfort of their passengers is not interfered with.

Some trains for the branch connected with a coach slipped from ex-London expresses at Harpenden station. This arrangement allowed the rear coach to be uncoupled whilst the train was in motion. It then coasted into the platform, controlled by the guard. In December 1906 a St Pancras train slipped its coach as usual at 4.39 pm, but for some reason the engine of the express braked hard and the slipped coach ran into the back of the train with some force, breaking lights and two windows. Several of the 30 passengers in the coach were injured when they collided with each other or got thrown around.

In spring 1907 special trains ran for the 7th Annual Show of Harpenden Agriculture & Fanciers' Association and on 19th June Harpenden Wesleyan Sunday School organised an outing to Hemel Hempstead. No less than 170 people left on the 1.43 pm train and returned at 9.50 pm. Another special train ran from Harpenden to Redbourn at 10.30 pm on 24th June, 1908, taking home supporters of the garden party and fete organised by the Tariff Reform League's Harpenden and Redbourn Branch.

In the opposite direction, a seaside excursion, organised by Revd W.K. Weston of Boxmoor, left Heath Park at 5 am on 30th June, 1908, arriving at Yarmouth at 10.40 am, and returned to Heath Park at 1 am (cost just 5s.).

A less successful 'special' (using the Pullman car train) ran from Hemel Hempstead to Harpenden at 10 pm on Wednesday 19th August, 1908, following the Hemel Hempstead Flower Show and Sports. On board were only 6 passengers (4 for Redbourn and 2 for Harpenden), and as the Show Committee had guaranteed the railway a £2 revenue for running the train, the Society had to dip into their own funds to make up the shortfall.

During 1908, in a show of compatibility, the Midland and LNWR agreed to accept each other's tickets in respect of journeys to Boxmoor or Hemel Hempstead stations, regardless of which route passengers chose to use.

Other excursions included one to Southend on Tuesday 28th June, 1910, organised by the Revd W.K. Wix. This left from Heath Park Halt at 7 am and picked up at Hemel Hempstead, but because 800 people boarded the train, four more coaches were added at Harpenden to relieve the overcrowding. A somewhat smaller party (169 members of the Mothers' Union) went from Harpenden to Redbourn, to take tea, on 5th July, 1910 and on 24th July, 1911 a 3.30 am departure from Hemel Hempstead conveyed people to Harpenden to view the Great Flying Race. Tickets, costing 1s. 3d., could not be booked at the station, but were available from Mr Day of Hemel Hempstead and Mr Edney of Boxmoor.

Rumours were rife in October 1911 that the LNWR and the Midland companies were considering a link-up at Boxmoor, but a month later a local proposition was put forward - for a triangle to be created by linking the Hemel Hempstead line to Apsley, via a new curve, with stations at Marlowes and Apsley; but neither materialised. Alterations were forced on the timetable in March 1912 because of a coal strike (some trains were withdrawn and others rescheduled) and also in that year the M&GN engines returned to their owners, whereupon Midland tank engines again worked the branch. The following year trailer car No. 2235, which was built for use with a steam railmotor, was converted into an ordinary 3rd class coach for use on the line. The provision of a brake compartment at either end reduced the seating to 40.

The onset of World War I forced more restrictions on branch working, but in the summer of 1916 a special train was arranged to leave Heath Park Halt at 11.44 am, carrying members of Hemel Hempstead Working Men's Club, their wives and children (33 adults and 51 children) to Luton for their annual outing. Trams were chartered to convey the party to Wardown Park for children's sports, before assembling at the Plait Hall for tea. Before leaving the tables, each child was presented with 3*d.*, which, together with tea expenses and railway fares, was met from Club funds. The party rejoined the branch and returned to Hemel Hempstead at about 8 pm after 'a very happy time'.

Not so happy were the passengers on the 7.45 pm train from Harpenden to Hemel Hempstead on 3rd February, 1917. One complained that when he tried to join the train, one carriage was already full and he was forced to travel in the guard's and goods' compartment, the floor of which was thickly coated with ice. 'To have to stand on this after a warmly heated London train is, to say the least, uncomfortable, and to older passengers risky from a health point of view', he argued. Apparently a number of munitions workers had taken to using the line and this was causing the overcrowding. The complainant ended 'it does not seem too much to expect the Company to provide adequate accommodation'. However, if he was on the train on 26th March, 1917 he would have been even less pleased, as it broke down near Redbourn and several Hempsteadians had to walk home!

As World War I ended, trains were having to take their place among other modes of transport and people were beginning to demand better services. Accordingly, in October 1920, Hemel Hempstead Council held a debate on bus and rail services in the town, during which the perennial call for trains to carry on to Boxmoor station re-emerged. The proposer had heard 'that the rails still existed and could be found if the rubbish was cleared away'. What he said was not true, but it did not matter because yet again no action followed the talk.

However, to enable pressure to be put on the two railway companies, a Season Ticket Holders' Association was formed for the Hemel Hempstead district on 28th January, 1921. A Committee of six was elected and the subscription set at 2*s.* 6*d.* By the following July the Association was reporting 'good progress' with the railway authorities and that 'they are showing a sympathetic tendency to meet the requirements of their clients', although no specific examples of this co-operation were quoted.

By the early 1920s the service still comprised seven trains a day in each direction on weekdays only, and on 21st April, 1921 0-4-4T engines Nos. 1254 and 1385 were working the branch, hauling coaches Nos. 276 and 421 respectively. Redbourn Parish Council, in October 1921, considered the service to be inadequate and petitioned the Midland asking for a 'pre-war service' to be reinstated.

Two months later the Season Ticket Holders' Association were also in contact with the Midland, raising the problems of morning and afternoon train timings which meant children arrived too early for school, and after school had a long wait for their return train. The Midland agreed to look into the matter, but it would appear this problem was never satisfactorily resolved, because on 19th October, 1937 Harpenden Council was voicing concern that children travelling to Hemel Hempstead always arrived late, missing assembly and part of a

A 1920 view of Hemel Hempstead station with a Midland 0-6-0T on a passenger train, the engine shed is obscured but can be seen extreme right. *Authors' Collection*

Ex-MR 0-6-0T No. 1669 on a 2-coach train at Hemel Hempstead on 19th October, 1929. *H.C. Casserley*

No. 1674 at Connor's Crossing with a train for Hemel Hempstead, 19th September, 1931. *J. Kite*

A Johnson '3F' 0-6-0T (fitted with condensing apparatus for working through the Metropolitan tunnels in the London area) is seen on an eastbound train after crossing the bridge over the Luton main road (then the A6 now the A1081) in 1935. *J.M. Jarvis*

An LMS Garratt is seen on a northbound train of empty coal wagons as it approaches Harpenden station in April 1935. The Hemel Hempstead train is seen to the right by the water column. *J.M. Jarvis*

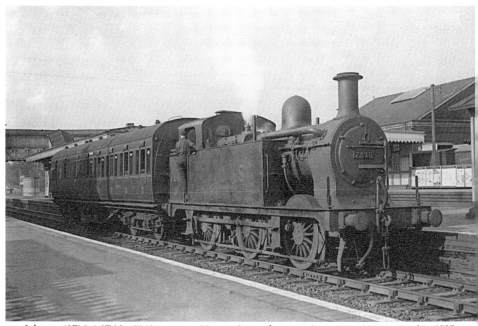

Johnson '3F' 0-6-0T No. 7248 is seen at Harpenden with a train from Hemel Hempstead in 1935.
J.M. Jarvis

Johnson '1F' 0-6-0T No. 1811, the Hemel Hempstead branch locomotive in Harpenden yard on 8th April, 1938.
J.M. Jarvis

lesson. They recommended that the train should start 15 minutes earlier and run on to Heath Park Halt.

By October 1925 the LMS was trying to attract regular passengers and introduced 3rd class weekly season tickets between Bedford and St Albans, including all the branch stations and halts. The weekly fares (Sunday to Saturday) were 15s. 7d. from Heath Park Halt, 15s. 3d. from Hemel Hempstead, 14s. 10d. from Godwin's Halt and 13s. 5d. from Beaumont's Halt and Redbourn.

The first few years of LMS ownership passed with little change but by the late 1920s efforts were being made throughout the region to cut expenditure and use their resources efficiently. A proposal was made for the passenger service on the branch to be withdrawn and Boxmoor station renamed 'Hemel Hempstead' (both stations were under LMS control by this time). This suggestion was debated by the Council in July 1928 when concern was voiced that there would then be two stations with the same name. Subsequently a suggestion was made for the old Midland station to be renamed 'Adeyfield', and later still 'Hemel Hempstead North', but as a passenger service was continued none of these ideas proved necessary.

However, from 4th March, 1929 the passenger service was reduced to one train morning and evening, with two trains during the day on Saturdays. This was because of the popularity of the LMS bus service (*see Chapter Nine*). Continuing with economies, the bay platform at Harpenden was closed from 2nd April, 1933. Harpenden North signal box was abolished soon afterwards and a new Harpenden Station signal box was built to replace the former Harpenden South signal box.

The LMS continued to run this abridged service of trains until, due to a coal shortage, the service was 'temporarily suspended' on 16th June, 1947. Apparently passenger numbers had dwindled during the previous 12 months until the only 'regulars' from the Harpenden end were six schoolchildren. Whereas they arrived late when using the train, by transferring to the 8.03 am bus from Harpenden station, they reached school in plenty of time. Season ticket holders were allowed to travel on the bus until their tickets expired. The authorities let it be known that re-opening of the passenger train service would depend on the fuel situation and public demand. In fact, space was reserved in timetables for a few years after, but the passenger service was never re-instated. Goods trains, however, continued to run and a variety of rolling stock found its way onto the branch.

From around 1940 some Fowler 2-6-2 tanks with condensing apparatus came to the line (Nos. 22/40 being noted), while later on the Stanier version of the 2-6-2 tanks saw use working mainly passenger trains, on which the guard issued tickets in bus-conductor style. Nos. 79, 91, 92, 98, 99, 111, 114, 148, 149, 155, 160, 161, 164 and 167 were noted.

Goods traffic was handled mainly by '3F' 0-6-0, No. 3245 (BR No. 43245) for many years, but the following engines were also observed: No. 58158 in 1950, and '3Fs' Nos. 43211, 43246, 43261, 43295, 43307, 43313, 43378, 43400, 43408, 43440, 43448, 43565, 43629, 43764, 43766, 43782, 43801 and 43806. Class '4F' No. 43888 came early in 1954 to handle the heavier trains, but sister engines also appeared, namely Nos. 43909, 44051, 44195 and 44530.

Johnson '3F' 0-6-0 No. 43261 is seen on the 3.12 pm Harpenden-Hemel Hempstead goods train near Roundwood Halt on 28th July, 1949. *H. Clements*

Fowler '4F' 0-6-0 No. 44581 is seen at Cotterells Sidings. *A.D. Edwards*

Ivatt 'Mogul' No. 43119 is about to join the Hemel Hempstead branch at Harpenden Junction, 1st October, 1955. *John Wood*

Johnson '3F' 0-6-0 No. 43245 at Harpenden on the Locomotive Club of Great Britain special on 11th May, 1957.   *Authors' Collection*

On the same day No. 43245 is seen passing Roundwood Halt.   *Authors' Collection*

A final view of '3F' No. 43245 on the LCGB special at Cotterells Sidings on 11th May, 1957.

A. Turner

Ivatt class '4MT' 2-6-0 No. 43120 is seen approaching Ambrose Lane bridge with a goods train in 1958.

A. Turner

Ivatt class '4' 2-6-0s were allocated to St Albans and No. 43118 came to the branch on 29th June, 1955, to be followed by Nos. 43019, 43031, 43119, 43120, 43121 and 43160, before No. 43119 became the regular engine. However, this engine suffered a derailment at St Albans Shed, which necessitated repairs at Derby, before returning to the branch on 2nd May, 1959. With the end of steam in sight, St Albans Shed closed on 11th January, 1960, and thereafter branch engines were supplied from Cricklewood. The first diesel appeared on 10th September, 1962, being No. D5395 (27 107).

This chapter would not be complete without a mention of the special trains which traversed the branch, after withdrawal of passenger services. On Saturday 30th May, 1948 a train, carrying 80 collectors and treasurers of the West Herts Hospital Contributary Scheme, left Harpenden at 5.35 pm, hauled by engine No. 43245, for Hemel Hempstead. More people joined the train at Redbourn and the party continued on to the Guild House at Apsley, where they were addressed by the President of the Hospital, Sir Walter Halsey. The train driver on this occasion was Mr H. Freeman, and the guard Mr H. Williams.

Several enthusiasts' specials travelled the line, the first being on 11th May, 1957, when Locomotive Club of Great Britain members were hauled by No. 43245 to Heath Park and back. The special train arrived at Harpenden's Platform 1 at 2.20 pm and Driver Victor Irish and Fireman Malcolm Gazely showed people over the footplate. A few minutes before departure time it was discovered that some intending passengers had not been able to alight at Harpenden and had been taken on to Luton. There a Derby to London express was stopped to pick them up, and meanwhile the special train was emptied and moved into the down fast siding, eventually emerging, after the express had departed, to start the 'special tour'. Despite the rain many spectators turned out to see the train on the branch.

No. 43245 hauled another special on 10th August, 1958, organised by the Railway Correspondence & Travel Society, called the 'Northern and Eastern Railtour', this being the last passenger train to Heath Park. Unusually, it went onto the branch tender-first. On 8th March, 1959 a weedkiller train made a much-needed trip up the line as far as Hemel Hempstead station.

Being a line with little traffic, not far from London, the branch was an ideal location for the Ministry of Transport to carry out tests on flares, a prototype tail lamp and a prototype detonator placer. On Monday 9th January, 1961 the 6.50 am goods train ran as usual, but its crew was asked to ensure clearance of the line by 11.30 am. Trains timed for 9.58 am and 1.30 pm were cancelled but a special train left Harpenden for Hemel Hempstead at 4 pm to cater for Dickinson's paper traffic. These alterations allowed time for a special train carrying MOT and railway officials to inspect the line prior to testing. On the Tuesday a road journey was made from Harpenden at 9 am. to fix a telephone at each test location and to fix the prototype tail lamp on a post alongside an ordinary one, and beamed to a point 200 yards away, near the Motorway bridge, with another pair erected at Roundwood Halt. The prototype detonator placer had previously been connected to the 3-lever ground frame at Hemel Hempstead at the goods yard points.

On 11th January a two-car dmu left St Pancras at 11.55 am for Harpenden,

The South Beds Locomotive Club special on 24th September, 1960 with Fowler class '3MT' 2-6-2T No. 40026 in charge. Seen here at Redbourn station.   *Authors' Collection*

Another view of the same train, this time at Hemel Hempstead.   Notice the condensing apparatus fitted to this engine , enabling it to work the Moorgate line.   *Authors' Collection*

where it joined a catering coach in the down fast siding. The dmu left at 2 pm and travelled over the branch testing the flares and inspecting the detonator placer, before returning to the siding at Harpenden at 4.03 pm, where welcome refreshment was taken from the catering coach - it was a very cold day! The next trip left in darkness at 5.10 pm. Again Brocks flares and USA flares were tested, and the tail lamps were viewed from a moving train. On the return more tests were undertaken in different circumstances, such as curved and straight track, on embankments and in cuttings. The lamps were collected up *en route* and the dmu ran straight back to St Pancras.

The South Beds Locomotive Club ran the next special on 24th September, 1960, carrying 285 passengers in four coaches, hauled by No. 40026. It departed from Harpenden at 2.17 pm, stopping at the halts and stations, and spent 1½ hours at Hemel Hempstead so that passengers could walk to the gasworks over the then closed part of the line. The train, driven by Mr R. MacGregor of Bedford, left at 4.50 pm, arriving back at Harpenden at 5.33 pm. One lad had full value for his 6s. 6d. ticket, as he was given the reporting numbers from the engine.

The following day (25th) members of Hemel Hempstead Model Railway Society joined a 4-car dmu at their end of the branch, for a one-way trip down the line as part of a round tour.

A 4-car dmu hauls the Hemel Hempstead Model Railway Society railtour on 26th September, 1960. It is seen here about to rejoin the main line at Harpenden Junction.

Authors' Collection

B 9069
(B) L. & N. W. Ry.
Road Motor Car Ticket.

| Boxmoor Station. |
| Heath Park Halt. |
| Bridge Street. |
| Hemel Hempstead. |

This Ticket is issued subject to the conditions in the Company's Time Table, Books, Bills, and Notices, is only available to the place marked by the Bell Punch, and must be shewn on demand. Passengers should not accept Tickets unless passed (through the Bell Punch) in their presence.

The LNWR horse bus at Boxmoor. *Top, right:* A ticket for the LNWR motor bus service which replaced the horse bus.

Authors' Collection

Chapter Nine

Horse to Horsepower

The situation at the Boxmoor end of the Harpenden to Hemel Hempstead Railway at the time of opening was well summed up by the *Hertford Mercury* as follows:

> This local line has at present very little connection with the LNWR - the first Act permitted goods only to be conveyed upon it. The 2nd Act allowed an alteration in route and the extension to Harpenden permits passengers to be carried from Harpenden to Hemel Hempstead, but did not grant a licence to carry passengers from Hemel Hempstead to Boxmoor Station. Consequently that part of the line so far as passengers are concerned is a nullity.

Whilst the LNWR were unable, or unwilling, to co-operate with the Midland Railway Company, insofar as a joint station was concerned, they were well aware, once the Midland line opened, that passengers were being lost in that direction. The main reason was that the Midland station was accessible to the townspeople of Hemel Hempstead, whereas the LNWR station was a long way away across the Moor. In an attempt to bridge this gap, and to poach customers away from the Midland line onto their own, the LNWR introduced a horse-drawn omnibus service between the two stations. This commenced on 2nd October, 1882 and was described at the time as 'a handsome omnibus, with handsome horses and a stately driver in handsome livery'.

In fact, two horse-drawn carriages were used (one slightly smaller than the other and pulled by only one horse). Fares related to distance travelled (e.g. from the town to Lower Marlowes cost 4*d.* and from Boxmoor station to Moor End 3d.), but even so many travellers felt the service was expensive. A railway posting house was established in Cheapside, where the 'buses' called to collect goods and parcels for the railway. Although it received a mixed reception from the travelling public, the horse-drawn service continued to run for a number of years. However, in June 1883 it ran into, and damaged, a Highways Committee wheelbarrow, whereupon 5*s.* was demanded for its repair.

Competition for the LNWR Horse Bus arrived on Monday 1st February, 1901, when the Hemel Hempstead Motor Car Company (run by Messrs Pemsel & Wilson) inaugurated a motor waggonette service between Boxmoor station and the town. The Mayor was one of the first passengers and the standard fare was 3*d.*, regardless of distance travelled. At this time motor vehicles were somewhat rare in the town and the service came about with much publicity and acclaim. Sadly, two days later the vehicle (named *Pilot*) was kept off the road because it had frozen up! In March a more powerful waggonette (named *Shamrock*) was collected from Kings Lynn in dreadful snowy weather. It was used mainly for excursions but sometimes shared the town service with *Pilot*, and was particularly useful when *Pilot*'s dashboard caught fire on 29th January, 1902, forcing its removal from service for a month.

To celebrate the first anniversary of the service, it was announced that no fares would be collected, but passengers were asked to put 3*d*. or more in the box provided on the vehicle, as a donation to the local Boer War Fund. £1 10*s*. was collected and *Shamrock* did all the trips. In the spring of 1902 a more comfortable and powerful 9 bhp Daimler waggonette (named *Rose*) was added to the fleet. She had solid rubber tyres and was capable of speeds up to 20 mph, but the company was anxious that they could not find a suitable coachhouse for their three cars.

The motors ran very successfully, but in September 1902 some of their regular passengers were upset at the withdrawal of one of the evening services, so much so that it was reinstated in November. In fact, a much improved service was introduced at this time, with both *Pilot* and *Shamrock* running. To provide more comfortable accommodation for the winter, a new body (made by Mr T. Christmas of Hemel Hempstead) had been put on *Shamrock*. This presumably closed in the seating - previously the motor looked like a large vintage car with a canopy and curtains.

However, at 11.30 am on 6th May, 1903 the company's good record was somewhat tarnished when one of the motors suffered a wheel collapse on the 'newly metalled road near Boxmoor Church'. All the passengers were shaken up, but the Revd Tatton, who had been sitting immediately above the wheel, came off worst. Nevertheless, the service continued and in February 1904 celebrated its third anniversary and looked fit to carry on. But at the beginning of 1905 the local press carried no timetable, nor did it mention the regular bus service or any excursions being run by the company. From this, it would appear, the vehicles were no longer up to the job and, therefore, passengers had to resort to the LNWR horse omnibus, which was still running.

In July 1905 Hemel Hempstead Council was aware of the poor communications systems available to residents and obviously felt the horse omnibus to be somewhat out of date, because they asked the LNWR what they were doing about a motor bus service for the town. It was suggested at this meeting that the Midland Railway Company should also be approached, but one councillor commented that 'the Midland had treated Hemel Hempstead no better than a village and haven't considered passengers at all', and further 'there is no point asking them for any further assistance'. The Council, at one stage, considered a 6 mile-long tramway system 'but that is for later', it decided. In the meantime, consideration was given to the Council running its own service of motor buses, but, deep down, it was probably highly relieved when it eventually heard from the LNWR that something was happening in that direction.

Meanwhile the horse omnibus carried on, unopposed but not uneventfully. On 31st October, 1905 it was leaving Boxmoor station when it was involved in a collision with a pony and trap, whose driver had not stopped because he assumed the omnibus would turn in the opposite direction. The pony got tangled in its reins but little damage was done. Two days later the omnibus was again in collision with a pony and trap, this time in the High Street, and on 1st February, 1906 one of the omnibus horses received a severely cut nose in a crash with a chauffeur-driven car. The omnibus was not damaged, and continued its journey with a fresh horse.

Early in the 1900s the LNWR began experimenting with motor buses, with a view to introducing them as horse omnibus replacements, and eventually, as promised to Hemel Hempstead Council, one came from Watford to be tried on the Boxmoor route. Because Marlowes Road was 'found to be sound for travelling purposes' a new service was planned to start on 4th November, 1907, but this did not materialise.

By June 1908 the Council was getting very upset by the lack of a motor bus, mainly because it had repaired the roads, as requested, but it was not until 28th July, 1909 that a specially constructed single-deck motor bus brought real hope of a service. During its trials, the vehicle was found to be capable of taking all the corners satisfactorily, with the result that the LNWR introduced it into service on Monday 9th August, making 21 journeys each day, and meeting all trains. Luggage and post office mails were carried on top and in April 1910 half-price fares for children were introduced. From June that year some runs were timetabled to Piccotts End.

Successful as the service was, the LNWR declined to provide a bus shelter at Boxmoor station in October 1911. They did, however, have to provide some spare parts for their bus, after it ran into Messrs Dickinsons' car on 22nd May, 1913, causing damage to both vehicles and shaking up the passengers, and also after it ran into a car near the 'Prince's Arms' on a foggy day in November. On this occasion the car sustained some minor damage, as did the bus chassis - and the bus starting handle was bent.

Whilst most railway bus services were withdrawn during World War I, this one maintained a service, but 'Friday the 13th' (July 1917) proved an unlucky one for its driver, Robert Squires. As the 3.5 pm bus stopped at Heath Park, he heard the sound of falling glass and on investigation, was told by his conductress, Miss Dorothy Cooper, that a window had been smashed by a very drunken passenger, Joseph Allen of London. Squires approached Allen to discuss the matter and was immediately punched in the face. At the Court case which followed, Allen pleaded guilty and was fined 10s. for damage to the bus, £1 for assault and £3 3s. costs.

When Hemel Hempstead's two railways came under LMS control in 1923 the LNWR bus was also absorbed into the bus system and, rather than link the two lines, the latter decided to continue running the bus as a cheaper option. In mid-August 1925 the vehicle was taken into 'dock' for improvements to be made and a Pioneer No. 4 char-a-banc was used instead. It was not long back in service when, on Wednesday, 11th November, it made an unscheduled stop - in the River Bulbourne! The driver (again Robert Squires) had taken action to avoid two cyclists when his bus was struck, while travelling at 12 mph, and sent off-course by an on-coming car. Squires resolutely steered his crowded bus (on two wheels at times) across a path, down the bank and into the river, proceeding along the river bed until the vehicle stuck in the soft mud. Fortunately it did not overturn and his passengers escaped with a few relatively minor injuries. Planks were obtained and put across the river to the bus for passengers to get out and a gang came from Watford, with ropes and lorry, to pull out the stricken vehicle. This proved impossible, so there it remained until

Card CL 3. L. 695

L M S ROAD AND RAIL SERVICES

22nd SEPT., 1930, and until further notice.

BUS SERVICE BETWEEN HEMEL HEMPSTED & BOXMOOR STATION, HEMEL HEMPSTED TOWN, REDBOURN, AND HARPENDEN

(Condition of Roads and other circumstances permitting.)

MONDAYS TO FRIDAYS.

	a.m.	A a.m.	a.m.	a.m.	a.m.	a.m.	a.m.	a.m.	a.m.	a.m.	B a.m.	A a.m.	B a.m.	B a.m.	B a.m.	B a.m.	a.m.	a.m.	a.m.	p.m.	p.m.	B p.m.	B p.m.	B p.m.	
Hemel Hempsted & Boxmoor Station, L M S ... ... dep.	5 30	6 0	6 15	6 55	6 50	7 25	7 44	8 5	8 10	8 25	9 0	9 0	9 45	10 32	10 50	11 15	11 25	11 40	11 55	12 50	1 5	2 20	2 55	3 15	...
Apsley Mills ... ... ,,	...	...	...	...	...	...	...	...	...	...	...	...	...	...	...	...	...	...	...	...	...	...	...	...	...
Hemel Hempsted (B'way) ,,	5 40	6 20	6 25	7 5	7 0	7 35	7 52	8 15	8 18	8 35	9 10	9 10	9 55	10 40	11 0	11 25	11 35	11 50	12 5	1 0	1 15	2 30	3 5	3 25	...
,, ,, (Mid. Rd.) ,,			6 27	7 7								9 12				11 27				1 2				3 27	...
Redbourn, Saracen's Head ,,	...	...	6 44	7 20	...	...	...	...	...	...	...	9 32	...	...	...	11 47	...	...	...	1 22	...	...	...	3 47	...
Harpenden Station, L M S arr.	...	...	6 57		...	...	...	...	...	...	...	9 45	...	...	...	12 0	...	...	...	1 35	...	...	...	4 0	...

	B p.m.	p.m.	F p.m.	A p.m.	A p.m.	A p.m.	F p.m.	A p.m.	p.m.	FX p.m.	FX p.m.	A p.m.	A p.m.	A p.m.	A p.m.	A p.m.	A p.m.	A p.m.	A p.m.	A p.m.	A p.m.	A p.m.	A p.m.	A p.m.	W Night
Hemel Hempsted & Boxmoor Station, L M S ... ... dep.	3 42	4 0	4 35	4 40	4 50	5 3	...	5 30	5 30	5 30	5 45	5 50	6 5	6 20	6 30	6 42	7 0	7 22	7 35	8 10	8 50	9 55	10 50	11 10	12 22
Apsley Mills ... ... ,,	...	...	5 5	...	...	...	5 5	...	...	6 5	6 5	...	...	...	...	...	...	...	...	...	...	...	...	...	...
Hemel Hempsted (B'way) ,,	3 50	4 10	5 15	4 50	5 0	5 13	5 15	...	5 40	6 15	6 15	6 0	6 15	6 30	6 40	6 52	7 10	7 32	7 45	8 20	9 0	10 5	11 0	11 20	12 30
,, ,, (Mid. Rd.) ,,			5 17				5 17	D		6 17	6 17				6 42				7 47						...
Redbourn, Saracen's Head ,,	...	...	5 30	...	...	...	5 37	...	...	6 30	6 30	...	...	...	7 2	...	...	...	8 7	...	...	...	...	...	...
Harpenden Station, L M S arr.	...	...	N	...	...	...	5 50	...	...	N	6 43	...	...	...	7 15	...	...	...	8 20	...	...	...	...	...	...

SATURDAYS.

	a.m.	A a.m.	a.m.	a.m.	a.m.	a.m.	a.m.	a.m.	a.m.	B a.m.	A a.m.	B a.m.	a.m.	B a.m.	a.m.	a.m.	a.m.	p.m.	A p.m.	p.m.	p.m.	A p.m.	A p.m.	p.m.	B p.m.
Hemel Hempsted & Boxmoor Station, L M S ... ... dep.	5 30	6 0	6 15	6 55	6 50	7 25	7 44	8 5	8 25	9 0	9 0	9 45	...	10 50	11 20	11 45	11 45	...	12 30	1 5	1 5	1 35	1 55	...	2 20
Apsley Mills ... ... ,,	...	...	...	...	...	...	...	...	...	...	...	...	...	...	...	12 5	...	12 5	...	...	...	...	...	...	...
Hemel Hempsted (B'way) ,,	5 40	6 20	6 25	7 5	7 0	7 35	7 52	8 15	8 35	9 10	9 10	9 55	10 30	11 0	11 30	12 15	11 55	12 15	12 40	...	1 15	1 45	2 5	...	2 30
,, ,, (Mid. Rd.) ,,			6 27	7 7							9 12		10 32			12 17		12 17		E				...	2 32
Redbourn, Saracen's Head ,,	...	...	6 44	7 20	...	...	...	...	...	...	9 32	...	10 52	...	...	12 30	...	12 37	...	...	...	...	...	2 0	2 52
Harpenden Station, L M S arr.	...	...	6 57		...	...	...	...	...	...	9 45	...	11 5	...	...		...	12 50	...	...	...	...	...	2 15	3 5

	A p.m.	p.m.	p.m.	p.m.	p.m.		p.m.	p.m.	p.m.	p.m.	A p.m.	p.m.	A p.m.	A p.m.	p.m.	A p.m.	A p.m.	p.m.	A p.m.	p.m.	A p.m.	A p.m.	A p.m.	A p.m.	Night
Hemel Hempsted & Boxmoor Station, L M S ... ... dep.	2 30	2 55	3 15	3 43	4 0	...	4 40	5 3	5 25	5 40	6 20	...	6 50	7 22	...	7 45	8 10	...	8 50	...	9 15	9 55	10 50	11 10	12 22
Apsley Mills ... ... ,,	...	...	...	...	...	...	...	...	...	...	...	...	...	...	...	...	...	...	...	...	...	...	...	...	...
Hemel Hempsted (B'way) ,,	2 40	3 5	3 25	3 50	4 10	...	4 50	5 13	5 35	5 50	6 30	6 35	7 0	7 32	7 35	7 55	8 20	8 20	9 0	9 5	9 25	10 5	11 0	11 20	12 30
,, ,, (Mid. Rd.) ,,			3 27			...	4 52		5 37			6 37			7 37			8 22		9 7					...
Redbourn, Saracen's Head ,,	...	...	3 47	...	...	...	5 12	...	5 55	...	...	6 57	...	...	7 57	...	...	8 42	...	9 27	...	...	...	...	...
Harpenden Station, L M S arr.	...	...	4 0	...	...	...	5 25	...	6 10	...	...	7 10	...	...	8 10	...	...	8 55	...	9 40	...	...	...	...	...

SUNDAYS.

	a.m.	A a.m.		A p.m.	A p.m.	A p.m.	A p.m.	A p.m.		A p.m.	A p.m.		A p.m.	A p.m.	A p.m.	A p.m.	A p.m.		A p.m.	A p.m.		A p.m.	A p.m.		
Hemel Hempsted & Boxmoor Station, L M S ... ... dep.	10 25	11 15	...	1 0	2 35	3 0	3 20	4 5	...	4 30	5 0	...	6 5	6 30	7 5	7 45	8 0	...	8 15	9 15	...	10 5	10 40	...	...
Apsley Mills ... ... ,,	...	...	...	...	...	...	...	...	...	...	...	...	...	...	...	...	...	...	...	...	...	...	...	...	...
Hemel Hempsted (B'way) ,,	10 35	11 25	...	1 10	2 45	3 10	3 30	4 15	...	4 40	5 10	...	6 15	6 40	7 15	7 55	8 10	...	8 25	9 25	...	10 15	10 50	...	...
,, ,, (Mid. Rd.) ,,		11 27	...	1 12				4 17	...			...	6 17				8 12	...			...			...	...
Redbourn, Saracen's Head ,,	...	11 47	...	1 32	...	...	...	4 37	...	...	...	...	6 37	...	...	...	8 32	...	...	...	...	...	...	...	...
Harpenden Station, L M S arr.	...	12 0	...	1 45	...	...	...	4 50	...	...	...	...	6 50	...	...	...	8 45	...	...	...	...	...	...	...	...

MONDAYS TO FRIDAYS.

	A a.m.	A a.m.	A a.m.	a.m.	a.m.	a.m.	a.m.	a.m.	a.m.	a.m.	a.m.	B a.m.	a.m.	B a.m.	B a.m.	B a.m.	B p.m.	p.m.	p.m.	p.m.	B p.m.	p.m.	p.m.	B p.m.	B p.m.
Harpenden Station, L M S dep.	...	...	...	...	...	7 10	...	...	...	...	...	...	9 55	...	...	...	...	...	12 22	...	...	2 0	...	...	...
Redbourn, Saracen's Head ,,	...	...	...	...	7 23	7 23	...	...	...	...	...	...	10 8	...	...	...	...	...	12 35	...	...	2 13	...	...	...
Hemel Hempsted (Mid. Rd.) ,,	...	...	...	...	7 43	7 43	...	...	...	...	...	...	10 28	...	...	...	...	...	12 55	...	...	2 33	...	...	...
,, ,, (B'way) ,,	5 45	6 22	7 15	7 35	7 45	7 45	7 52	8 15	8 20	8 40	9 17	10 15	10 30	10 40	11 15	11 35	12 5	12 40	12 57	2 0	2 35	2 40	3 20	3 50	4 10
Apsley Mills ... ... ,,	...	...	...	...	7 55	8 0	...	...	...	...	...	...	...	...	...	...	...	...	...	...	...	...	...	...	...
Hemel Hempsted & Boxmoor Station, L M S ... ... arr.	5 55	6 32	7 25	7 43	8 0	8 10	8 0	8 25	8 30	8 50	9 27	10 25	10 40	10 50	11 25	11 45	12 15	12 50	1 10	2 10	2 45	2 50	3 30	4 0	4 20

	p.m.	FX p.m.	F p.m.	p.m.	p.m.	F p.m.	F p.m.	p.m.	p.m.	p.m.	p.m.	F p.m.	FX p.m.	p.m.	FX p.m.	FX p.m.	F p.m.	p.m.	p.m.	p.m.	A p.m.	A p.m.	A p.m.	p.m.	p.m.
Harpenden Station, L M S dep.	...	4 15	4 15	...	...	...	N	...	...	...	...	6 0	N	...	...	6 45	...	...	7 25	...	...	8 40	...	...	...
Redbourn, Saracen's Head ,,	...	4 28	4 28	...	...	...	5 30	...	...	...	...	6 15	6 30	...	...	6 58	...	...	7 38	...	...	8 53	...	...	...
Hemel Hempsted (Mid. Rd.) ,,	...	4 48	4 48	...	...	H	5 48	...	...	...	...	6 45	6 47	...	...	7 18	...	...	7 58	...	...	9 13	...	...	...
,, ,, (B'way) ,,	4 50	4 50	4 50	5 5	5 15	...	5 50	5 50	6 0	6 15	6 30	6 47	6 49	7 5	7 10	7 20	7 20	7 33	8 0	8 30	9 5	9 15	10 20	11 0	11 20
Apsley Mills ... ... ,,	...	...	5 0	...	...	...	...	...	...	...	...	...	...	...	...	...	...	...	...	...	...	...	...	...	...
Hemel Hempsted & Boxmoor Station, L M S ... ... arr.	5 0	5 0		5 15	5 25	5 46	6 0	6 0	6 10	6 25	6 40	6 57	6 59	7 15	7 20	7 30	7 30	7 43	8 10	8 40	9 15	9 25	10 30	11 10	11 30

SATURDAYS.

	A a.m.	A a.m.	A a.m.	a.m.	a.m.	a.m.	a.m.	a.m.	a.m.	a.m.	a.m.	a.m.	B a.m.	B a.m.	a.m.	p.m.	p.m.	p.m.	p.m.	p.m.	p.m.	p.m.	p.m.	p.m.	p.m.
Harpenden Station, L M S dep.	...	...	...	...	...	7 10	...	...	...	...	...	9 55	...	...	11 10	...	...	...	...	...	1 30	...	...	...	...
Redbourn, Saracen's Head ,,	...	...	...	...	7 23	7 23	...	...	...	...	...	10 8	...	...	11 23	...	...	12 30	...	...	1 43	...	...	...	...
Hemel Hempsted (Mid. Rd.) ,,	...	...	...	...	7 43	7 43	...	...	...	...	...	10 28	...	...	11 38	...	...	12 47	C	...		...	...	...	...
,, ,, (B'way) ,,	5 45	6 22	7 15	7 35	7 45	7 45	7 52	8 15	8 40	9 17	10 30	10 31	11 20	11 35	11 40	12 5	12 40	12 50	...	1 15	...	2 0	2 10	2 40	3 5
Apsley Mills ... ... ,,	...	...	...	...	7 55	8 0	...	...	...	...	...		...	...	11 50	...	...	...	...	...	...	...	...	...	...
Hemel Hempsted & Boxmoor Station, L M S ... ... arr.	5 55	6 32	7 25	7 43	8 0	8 10	8 0	8 25	8 50	9 27	10 40	...	11 30	11 45		12 15	12 50	1 0	1 20	1 25	...	2 10	2 20	2 50	3 15

		p.m.	p.m.	B p.m.	B p.m.	p.m.		p.m.	p.m.	p.m.	p.m.	p.m.	p.m.	p.m.	p.m.	p.m.	p.m.	p.m.	A p.m.	A p.m.	A p.m.	A p.m.	p.m.	p.m.	p.m.
Harpenden Station, L M S dep.	...	2 45	3 10	...	...	4 15	...	...	...	5 45	...	6 30	...	...	...	7 25	...	8 25	...	...	9 10	...	10 15	...	...
Redbourn, Saracen's Head ,,	...	2 58	3 23	...	...	4 28	...	...	...	5 58	...	6 43	...	...	...	7 38	...	8 38	...	...	9 23	...	10 28	...	...
Hemel Hempsted (Mid. Rd.) ,,	...	3 18	3 43	...	...	4 48	...	...	...	6 18	...	7 3	...	...	...	7 58	...	8 58	...	...	9 43	...	10 48	...	...
,, ,, (B'way) ,,	...	3 20	3 45	3 50	4 20	4 50	...	5 15	5 50	6 20	6 30	7 5	7 5	7 33	7 55	8 0	8 30	9 0	9 0	9 30	9 45	10 30	10 50	11 0	11 20
Apsley Mills ... ... ,,	...	...	...	...	...	...	...	...	...		...		...	...	...		...		...	...	...	...	...	...	...
Hemel Hempsted & Boxmoor Station, L M S ... ... arr.	...	3 30	3 55	4 0	4 30	5 0	...	5 25	6 0	...	6 40	...	7 15	7 43	8 5	...	8 40	...	9 10	9 40	9 55	10 40	11 0	11 10	11 30

SUNDAYS.

	a.m.	A p.m.		A p.m.	A p.m.	A p.m.	A p.m.	A p.m.		A p.m.	A p.m.		A p.m.	A p.m.	A p.m.	A p.m.	A p.m.		A p.m.	A p.m.		A p.m.	A p.m.		
Harpenden Station, L M S dep.	...	12 10	...	1 45	...	...	...	...	...	...	5 13	...	...	...	7 10	...	...	...	...	9 10	...	...	...	...	...
Redbourn, Saracen's Head ,,	...	12 23	...	1 58	...	...	...	...	...	...	5 26	...	...	...	7 23	...	...	...	...	9 23	...	...	...	...	...
Hemel Hempsted (Mid. Rd.) ,,	...	12 43	...	2 18	...	...	...	...	...	...	5 36	...	...	...	7 43	...	...	...	...	9 43	...	...	...	...	...
,, ,, (B'way) ,,	10 40	12 45	...	2 20	2 50	3 10	3 40	4 40	...	5 10	5 48	...	6 40	7 20	7 45	8 0	8 50	...	9 25	9 45	...	10 15	10 50	...	...
Apsley Mills ... ... ,,	...	...	...	...	...	...	...	...	...	...	...	...	...	...	...	...	...	...	...	...	...	...	...	...	...
Hemel Hempsted & Boxmoor Station, L M S ... ... arr.	10 50	12 55	...	2 30	3 0	3 20	3 50	4 50	...	5 20	5 58	...	6 50	7 30	7 55	8 10	9 0	...	9 35	9 55	...	10 25	11 0	...	...

D—To Two Waters arrive 5.38 p.m. E—To Two Waters arrive 1.13 p.m. F—Fridays only. FX—Fridays excepted. N—These trips arrive at and depart from The Cricketers' Inn at Redbourn. H—Leaves Two Waters at 5.38 p.m. C—Leaves Two Waters at 1.15 p.m.

W—Wednesday Night only.

A—This bus runs via Two Waters. B—This bus runs via St. John's Road and Heath Park; all other buses run direct via Heath Park.

the following morning, when it was hauled out by a traction engine. It had a twisted chassis, very little glass and some other damage, but it was eventually sent to Wolverton for repair.

As time went by the LMS bus fleet was expanded nationally and construction of new buses released older Leyland Lions for other work. It was one of these which, on 18th February, 1929, commenced an extended service from Boxmoor station to Harpenden station, basically following the route of the LNWR omnibus and motor bus as far as Hemel Hempstead station, and then the route of the branch, but with eleven intermediate stops. Less than a month later the train service was reduced to two trains daily in each direction.

A bus timetable issued on 22nd September, 1930 shows 46 daily (weekday) departures from Boxmoor; eight going right through to Harpenden, two terminating at Redbourn and the rest providing a frequent local service between the station and the town centre. The first bus left at 5.30 am and the last bus at 11.10 pm, except on Wednesdays and Saturdays when a late bus left Boxmoor at 12.22 am, arriving at the town centre at 12.30 am.

No Sunday service had ever operated on the branch, but the LMS introduced a Sunday timetable for its bus service, running 18 departures from Boxmoor, with 5 going through to Harpenden. The fare from Boxmoor to Harpenden was 1s. 1d., but a variety of reduced tickets was offered, e.g. Workmen's, Market Tickets (on Thursdays only), Monthly Season Tickets and cheap combined omnibus and rail tickets to Luton. Certain tickets could be used on either buses or trains, but not Season Tickets, and holders of these petitioned the LMS, without success, in February 1930.

Mr Frederick James Odell did not have much success either, when he took the LMS to Court on 16th February, 1931. He had been riding his motorbike, on 4th December, 1929 at 7.30 am in Fish Street, Redbourn, when the LMS bus, which had just picked up passengers, pulled out and knocked him off his machine. Odell was propelled through a shop door and landed by the counter, suffering cuts and two broken fingers. He sued the LMS for personal injuries but the Court found against Odell for travelling too fast. At the end of the hearing the Clerk of the Court told him 'You have my sympathy', and it became known that the Judge was an LMS shareholder!

On the evening of 25th May, 1931 the LMS bus was again in an accident, this time colliding with a car driven by Mr Taylor of Harpenden on the Redbourn to Harpenden road.

Having operated the service as a satisfactory alternative to running trains, the LMS gave up ownership of the route in 1933, when it was taken over by the London Passenger Transport Board (later London Transport). It became Route 307 and in July 1956 buses began their journey from Westfield, Harpenden instead of from the station.

Meanwhile, on 12th July, 1934, the Hemel Hempstead Chamber of Commerce debated another grievance - this time from passengers who had been left stranded at Harpenden because the bus *had left dead on time*, and did not wait for the trains! 'Better co-operation between the railway and bus staffs should be insisted upon', they decided.

The Ro-Railer coach and a special train from London hauled by LMS 4-4-0 No. 556   for demonstration day, 22nd January, 1931, at Redbourn station.   *LMS Official*

The Karrier Ro-Rail motor-lorry at Redbourn on 22nd January, 1931.   *Real Photographs*

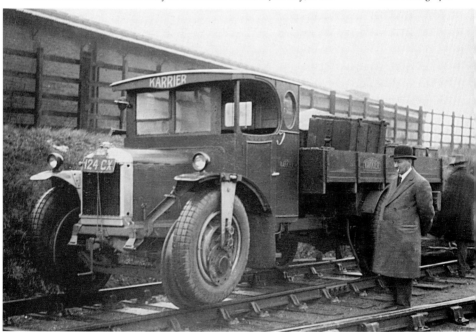

The Ro-Railer

In 1928 discussions took place between the LMS and Karrier Motors of Huddersfield, with the aim of producing a motor coach which could run on rails as well as on the road, in the hope of making more efficient use of branch lines. By the end of 1930 the prototype was delivered to Watford, from where it ran daily trials to Hemel Hempstead. There, it was driven round the town and then ran by rail to Redbourn, having joined the railway by means of a specially constructed ramp of sleepers laid between the tracks to provide a level base for the changeover from road to rail wheels. The 26-seater coach was fitted with buffers and rail couplings and could reach 60 mph on the road and 75 mph on the rails. Many railway officials attended the trials, and there being no real problems, a public demonstration was arranged for 22nd January, 1931.

A special train, hauled by a Midland Railway 4-4-0 No. 556, carried railway personnel from home and abroad, government officials and, of course, the press, along the branch to Redbourn, where it was put in a siding while the assembled company was entertained to luncheon aboard the train. Sir Josiah Stamp then gave a short speech, broadcast by loudspeakers throughout the train, in which he detailed what the party were about to see.

The Ro-Railer, as it became known, was standing ready for inspection and left on its first demonstration run at 1.30 pm. On arrival at Hemel Hempstead it went into the siding near Crescent Road, where the ramp had been laid, and was changed over to its road wheels in less than four minutes. It then drove out into Crescent Road, down Alexandra Road and Midland Road, and re-entered the station approach ready to start its return journey to Redbourn, which it reached in 9 minutes, travelling at 30 mph, and gave a smooth and comfortable ride. Three round trips were made so that all those interested could experience a ride.

Meanwhile, back at Redbourn, a Karrier motor-lorry, again with road and rail wheels, was on display, making short journeys along the siding. At the end of the headshunt an upturned sleeper had been used instead of a buffer, and the lorry did not stop in time and ran over the sleeper, becoming derailed beyond the end of the rails.

The engine which had brought the special train was moved along to the derailed lorry and a towrope attached. After several attempts, it was pulled back on the track - there being no shortage of officials to supervise the operation!

Well satisfied with their day out, the party returned to London. The Ro-Railer, however, left the area and in due course entered service for a short time at Stratford-Upon-Avon, before ending its days in Karrier's Luton depot.

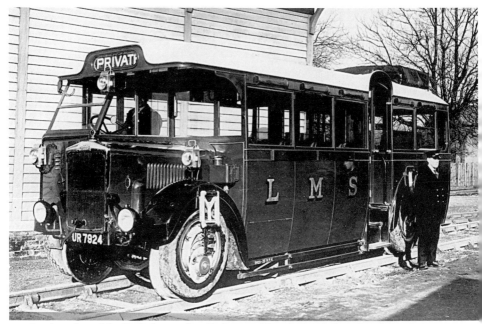

Another view of the Ro-Railer coach at Redbourn. Note the inside-keyed track.

Real Photographs

The Ro-Railer coach returning to Redbourn passing Wood End Lane bridge, 22nd January, 1931.

Authors' Collection

Chapter Ten

Goods Traffic

In describing the goods traffic carried on the Harpenden to Hemel Hempstead Railway, it will become obvious that this was a line dominated by the supply of coal, which was most likely the Midland Railway Company's objective from the outset. However, one must bear in mind that the line was only about nine miles long and there were only two 'proper' stations on it. This being so, the volume and variety of products carried proves how important the branch was to the communities it served, but this traffic did not pass directly on and off the railway at Harpenden Junction. Freight wagons for the branch were delivered to Harpenden goods yard, where they were sorted, ready for an engine to collect them.

Redbourn, being a village in the midst of an agricultural area, saw many different commodities coming and going through its goods yard. The yard had a capacity of 34 wagons, in three sidings - the long one being the coal siding. Another siding ran beside the goods shed and the third into the shed, which housed a 1 ton hand crane.

Different seasons brought different kinds of traffic to Redbourn, some bringing their own particular hazards. In the 1880s Messrs Russell & Harborough opened a jam and boiled sweet factory near to the station, and, although most of its products were distributed locally, some did get dispatched by rail. Although the incoming soft fruit (including raspberries from Scotland) and sugar brought trade to the branch, it also brought swarms of wasps which built their nests around the station.

Messrs Pipers had a building beside the line and dealt in animal offal etc. They toured the area with a large lorry, visiting abattoirs to collect their products and then sorted them for dispatch by rail. Fat was sent, in sacks, to Harris of Bow, soapmakers, hooves went for glue-making and bones for fertilizer. Pelts were cleaned before being tied into bundles and taken to the goods shed to be loaded by the crane into wagons. Pipers also dealt with large quantities of wool.

Harvest time saw a flurry of activity, with grain being dispatched from the many farms in the neighbourhood. A special platform was put up at the road doors of the goods shed to help with the unloading of carts and lorries. The small building at the end of the goods shed was intended as a goods office, but was used to store official railway-owned sacks, each bearing the name of the owning company. They were very large and could hold up to 2 cwt of grain. Farmers hired these from the railway (for ¼d. each per week in 1927) and obtained them in bundles of 20. Ninteen were folded in a special way so as to fit into the 20th sack. A vast amount of the grain handled at Redbourn was bought by Messrs Tooley of Luton (seed merchants). Other agricultural products dispatched from this station included hay and straw. Mr Dell of Leverstock Green went around the farms buying up hayricks etc., and branch staff dreaded seeing him doing business at the station because they knew there was some heavy loading ahead. The hay and straw was sent away in open wagons, sheeted over.

Ivatt 'Mogul' No. 43119 is seen at Redbourn on an up train, 22nd August, 1958. *C. Polkinghorne*

Sister engine No. 43118 drifts gently into Hemel Hempstead station with the goods train in May 1962. *S. Summerson*

Railway stables up and down the country operated a two-way traffic of their own, keeping some of the hay and straw and sending away manure. Wagons of the latter, as they arrived at Redbourn, were met with the order that they be immediately placed at the furthest end of the coal siding, well away from the station! For some time the person responsible for unloading the manure made sure there was a little left in the wagon, and he would come back later with his wheelbarrow to take it to his allotment behind the station. Apparently he grew superb onions!

In 1927 some 30 cwt of watercress a day was leaving Redbourn for London, Manchester and Liverpool, and in the same year a large quantity of bricks came in by rail for the council houses being built near Church End. These were carried to the site by local hauliers, Reddings. Small parcels were delivered within half a mile radius of the station by a porter using a handcart, although a cockerel is known to have travelled beyond that boundary on the back of a porter's bicycle.

About this time a huge machine was built on waste ground at the entrance to the station, into which was fed a mixture of granite chips and fine asphalt. A furnace was lit underneath and the end product used to resurface the stretch of A5 road between St Albans city boundary and the Bedfordshire border. All the raw materials for the work arrived on site via the branch.

At the 29½ milepost a private siding, known as Owen's Siding, was installed in 1894. Owen's, gravel merchants, had to repay the £290 cost at £29 for 10 years. It was situated on the up side of the line near the top of a short 1 in 86 gradient, but the siding was built level. The Midland Railway Company, therefore, gave an undertaking to the Board of Trade inspector that only up trains would shunt the siding, and he accordingly passed it for use on 20th September, 1894. It could accommodate about 8 wagons.

Owen's Siding had been unused for some time when, in September 1935, the siding rails were removed, together with the point leading into it, and the branch was re-joined with two lengths of rail mounted on LNWR and GCR chairs. The fact that the whole line was relaid, from the Hemel Hempstead end, in 1935, using LMS chairs, suggests Owen's Siding was lifted after that work had been done, with second-hand materials being used to fill the gap.

The Claydale Brick & Tile Company started near Cupid Green and in 1898 asked the Midland Railway for siding connections. The cost was estimated at £1,305, but the brick company offered to level the ground and pay £1,000 towards the cost. Plans were sent to the Board of Trade on 4th May, 1899 and the works were said to be almost ready by the end of September, but it was not until 30th January, 1900 that Col Von Donop inspected them. Several previous dates had been arranged but then cancelled. The one scheduled for 22nd November, 1899 was cancelled at the last minute when it was realised the timetable allowed only 10 minutes for the new works to be inspected!

The sidings were laid in the form of a passing loop with a centre siding, with connections into the works from the loop. Because of the steep gradient down from the sidings, an undertaking had to be given that no wagons of down trains would be left on the main line, but would be put into the centre siding provided for the purpose, while the rest were being shunted. This undertaking was sent to the Board of Trade on 1st March, 1900. In Claydale's early days mainly coal was brought in by rail, and they sent out some of their finished products. The clay for their bricks (which had 'Hemel Hempstead' moulded into them) came from nearby claypits via a 2 ft gauge tramway, but all evidence of this has disappeared under the industrial area of the New Town. In 1933 Brocks' Fireworks opened a factory at Cupid Green, and for a short time they used Claydale Sidings. As already mentioned, sidings were installed for Mr Godwin near Hemel Hempstead and these were used for coal and farm requirements. By 1884 more space was needed to accommodate the goods traffic here and in March of that year work started on preparing the site for an additional siding. During May the track arrived, and the total cost came to £182 19s. 11d. Thirty wagons could then be accommodated. Local coal merchants used the sidings as a coal depot and during World War II the Ministry of Supply built a warehouse adjoining the newest siding. At that time one or two trains a week would travel to the warehouse (which was taken over after the war by an engineering firm). A weighbridge was installed on this site in 1901.

The goods yard at Hemel Hempstead station, by its very situation, was a rather cramped affair, but latterly had space for about 50 wagons. Coal was its main commodity. Henry Balderson (one of the line's original Directors) was the first coal merchant to operate from the station. He had previously owned a coal business, then sold it, but hastily repurchased it and started trading again soon after the railway opened. Between May and July 1884 a new horse-dock and cattle pen was built here at a cost of £99 1s. 3d.

In the middle of the yard, the long siding was roofed over in 1896 to give protection to the products of Dickinson's paper mills, during loading. This traffic grew and some years later the LMS entered into a contract to deliver Dickinson's goods to towns in the Midlands and Northern England. From 1950 Dickinson's took large quantities of goods direct to Somerstown, London, by road, but they did not forsake the branch completely. In latter days eight or nine wagons left Hemel Hempstead every evening and when the train staff was handed over at Harpenden Junction a note was also passed to the signalman giving the destinations of these wagons, so that he could advise the Control Office.

Several other products were dealt with on a regular basis, though in smaller quantities. Watercress was one - this time from the Gade Valley growers. However, when BR decided it must be transported in complete wagon loads only, the trade was diverted to Boxmoor instead, but the new route took longer and eventually watercress returned to the branch, being carried in crates or baskets in a brake van, or, when no wagons were leaving, it travelled on the engine tender to Harpenden.

The Silicate Company, based next to Hemel Hempstead station, dispatched two or three wagons per week, mainly of grit and manure products. Incoming manure was unloaded on the short loop siding at the edge of the yard.

In December 1880, as a result of a meeting in Derby, the Midland and LNWR agreed to charge 2s. per ton for the cartage of ale within the town of Hemel Hempstead, regardless of which line it arrived on, and in 1906 the two companies reached agreement on the pooling of goods in the town. Initially a Midland van undertook all the cartage and there was no competition - in fact, relations between the two companies was said to be good. However, by 1911, public opinion observed that, since the pooling of goods, neither company cared about Hemel Hempstead and the service had deteriorated.

Up until the first week of September 1901 Hempsteadians were unable to purchase a newspaper before 8.15 am, at which time they arrived on the LNWR omnibus, but then newsagent Mr J. Brackett found that he could obtain his parcel of papers via the 6.45 am Midland train and have them on sale by 7 am which was much appreciated by all who left Hemel Hempstead early in the day. The following week Mr C.W. Floyd and other newsagents announced they were adopting the same practice!

From time to time Hemel Hempstead goods staff were called upon to deal with more unusual traffic, as in 1904 when a special train arrived from Scotland, conveying luggage, horses and carriages belonging to Mr John Kerr MP. This gentleman had arranged for his family to rent an impressive local property, Gaddesden Place, on a one-year tenure, but on 1st February, 1905 the building was gutted by fire and most of his property was lost. Following the fire, he temporarily lodged in the Railway Hotel at Boxmoor.

On 21st September, 1913 guns and other military equipment arrived at Hemel Hempstead for manoeuvres in the area, which must have made quite an impression on the local residents as the machinery was unloaded by a detachment of Royal Garrison Artillery and transported using 6-horse teams. More amazingly, in 1914 the Midland authorities received an application for the railway embankment just north of the station to be used as a butt for revolver practice!

World War I brought considerable problems to the Goods Department, but the general public were particularly hit by a meat shortage. On 3rd January, 1918 Hemel Hempstead Market had only two beasts for sale, one of which was so small 'it seemed a shame to slaughter it'. In accordance with legal requirements, the animals were taken to the Midland goods yard and weighed, whereupon the Auctioneer announced he would not offer them for sale, but they were reserved for local butchers.

By April 1919 local commerce was still struggling to get back to its pre-war efficiency, but it was hampered by the Midland's inefficiency. Mr G.A. Talbot MP tabled a question in the House of Commons, asking the President of the Board of Trade for suitable arrangements to be made to expedite delivery of goods from Hemel Hempstead station, because local tradespeople were incurring losses, owing to delays in transportation. The President, Mr Bridgeman, replied that he was in communication with the Midland Railway and would inform the Honourable Gentleman of the result. On 10th May the town's Mayor received a letter from the Midland saying that in the latter part of 1918 a reduction had been made in the company's cartage establishment due to the War, but steps were being taken to increase cartage facilities again and hoped there would shortly be no reasonable cause for complaint.

In 1920, when the spoils of World War I were distributed, Hemel Hempstead was awarded a tank as a reward for its war effort. This vehicle travelled via the branch to Cotterells Sidings, where, for a week, it attracted viewers young and old. It was necessary to bring it via the Midland route because this was nearest to its final site and, had it come via Boxmoor station it would have had to cross a river bridge which was considered to be of insufficient strength to bear the 27

Hemel Hempstead goods yard in 1960. *A.D. Edwards*

Ivatt 'Mogul' No. 43118 is seen shunting in Hemel Hempstead goods yard, 30th May, 1962.
S. Summerson

tons of tank.

At 3 pm on 21st February the tank left Cotterells under its own power, escorted by Dickinson's Silver Band, to its permanent site on a concrete base at Heath Park, where a handing-over ceremony was performed. (By 1923 the tank was in a very tatty state and the Council wanted to remove it, but, after a public outcry, decided to leave it alone. The British Legion then opened a fund to pay for it to be repainted!)

From time to time Hemel Hempstead goods yard was the venue for auction sales, one of which was held on Friday 15th April, 1921, when Messrs Rumball & Edwards disposed of 3,500 feet of sawn timber flooring and other timber, accumulated through the demolition of army huts by Messrs Potten & Co. Ltd of Luton, which , one assumes, was transported via the branch.

To understand the development of goods traffic between Hemel Hempstead and Boxmoor, it is necessary to delve into the history of the town's gas supply. We find that on 2nd January, 1873 (well before the Hemel Hempstead branch became operational), the small gas company at Two Waters, Boxmoor, agreed to purchase two 10-ton wagons (Order Nos. 14050/1) from the Gloucester Wagon Company, at a yearly rental of £19 per wagon, payable quarterly until £133 was paid, at which time the builder's plates could be removed and full ownership claimed. Referred to by the gas company as No. 1 and No. 2, they were delivered in early February. Although by this time a line had been built from Boxmoor as far as the town of Hemel Hempstead (which passed beside the gasworks), and it did have a connection to the LNWR goods yard, albeit by turntable, it is almost certain that these wagons did not transfer to the new stretch of railway.

Gasworks-bound coal was collected from the LNWR yard by private carters until January 1878, when the gas company accepted Mr Bradshaw's offer to cart coal from the new Midland station at 1s. per ton. In February he was paid £11 12s. but in January 1879 the rate was reduced to 9½d. per ton.

In 1880 the Boxmoor gasworks amalgamated with another Hemel Hempstead gasworks. The new company proposed to extend the Boxmoor works and install its own siding 'provided the Midland Railway Company would be prepared to supply coal that far'. The branch was open by this time, but the gas company's wish could only be granted by a Midland decision to use the derelict section of line beyond Hemel Hempstead station. On 17th February, 1880 Mr Allport replied to the gas company on behalf of the Midland Board, saying 'We shall undertake to convey all gas coals required for the Hemel Hempstead Gas Company to the sidings of the new works at Boxmoor at the same rate per ton as we are charging for the time being to Hemel Hempstead Midland Station'. A good offer, not to be refused! The gas company, anticipating that their wagons (which were fully paid for in January 1880) would be used on Midland lines, sent them away for checking and any necessary repairs.

Plans and estimates for the new siding were drawn up by the Midland's Way & Works Committee, and passed on 6th July, 1880. An amount of £150 was allowed by the railway company for construction of that part of the siding up to the gas company's boundary, with that company paying for the siding within their own boundaries. In addition, the gas company agreed to pay 10s. per chain, per annum, for use of that part of the siding which ran over railway

A Johnson '3F' is seen at Heath Park Halt while a No. 307 bus (formerly operated by the LMS) approaches, June 1952.

A. Willmott

A Johnson '3F' with a rake of coal wagons takes water at Hemel Hempstead station in 1949.

A. Willmott

company land. Further, the gas company was to pay for new rails, when needed, and all wagons were to be moved by Midland locomotives. The work was completed on 22nd December, 1880, at a cost of £187 7s. but the gas company was not happy with the work and complained to the Midland Board, whose workmen had carried it out. They replied that a contractor would not have done any better, but refrained from sending their bill until April 1881.

With the extra traffic generated by the gasworks, it soon became obvious that Hemel Hempstead station goods yard could not accommodate all the coal trucks, in addition to its normal goods traffic, and so the Midland company decided to utilise a piece of surplus land by Cotterells Road to provide extra handling facilities. There remained a stretch of embankment on this land (a left-over from Grover's abandoned short route) which only needed track and a connection to the branch, thus avoiding building formalities and major earthworks. On 28th February, 1882 the Midland General Purposes Committee approved an estimate of £300 for new sidings, and work started almost immediately. However, by taking up rails on the unused section between the gasworks and Roughdown Road bridge, the amount expended was much less than the estimate, as the following table of costs shows:

			£	s.	d.
March	-	Labour, groundwork	15	12	3
		Cranley Iron Co. - slag	1	0	0
		Engine	4	10	0
May	-	Labour, groundwork	27	2	7
		Engine	4	10	0
		Track, etc.	118	3	10
August	-	Carriage of Track	7	15	10
			178	14	6

(N.B. The reference to Cranley Iron Co. could have been a mistaken entry for Cranstone Iron Co., which was situated on the opposite side of the river from where the new sidings were being built. This would explain the small cost incurred.)

The finished work comprised a spur, which branched off near the Heath Park Hotel, and almost immediately divided into a passing loop as it descended the embankment. Re-formed as a single track, it ran a little way parallel with Cotterells Road, finally branching into two short sidings.

In October 1886, soon after the Midland Railway Company formally absorbed the Hemel Hempstead company, it was keen to establish ownership of its land and duly fenced off the section from Heath Park to Cotterells Sidings, without leaving access to a public footpath over the Moor. Once rights of way had been established by the Boxmoor Trustees, the Midland was forced to create a level crossing, complete with gates, over the line at the end of the passing loop. A goods shed was built, in 1890, by Brown & Sons, at a cost of £524 5s. 6d. (theirs being the lowest of seven tenders submitted). This straddled the shorter of the two sidings, nearest Cotterells Road, and overhung a roadway between the sidings, which allowed for loading to take place in the dry. Inside the shed was

A view of Cotterells Depot taken on 16th August, 1936. *Adrian Vaughan Collection*

Trip working No. 87, taken from the working timetable of September, 1957.

ST. ALBANS TRIP ENGINE.

No. 87.

Class 4F (2-6-0) Engine.

6.15 a.m. to 8.30 p.m. (S.X.), 2.15 p.m. (S.O.).

	arr. a.m.	dep. a.m.
St Albans Loco. Shed...	......	6 15 L.E.
Harpenden ...	6 25	7 2
Redbourn ...	7 16	7 30
Godwin's Halt	7*43	7*45
Hemel Hempsted	7 52	8 20
Redbourn ...	8 43	8 45
Harpenden ...	9 12	9 45
Redbourn ...	9 58	10 13
Godwin's Halt	10*26	10*28
Hemel Hempsted	10 35	10 55
Heath Park ...	11 2	11 7
Gas Works Sdgs.	11 13	11 40
		P.M.
Heath Park ...	11 47	12 35

Continued in next column.

No. 87—*continued.*

	arr. P.M.	dep. P.M.
Hemel Hempsted	12 42	1 10
Redbourn ...	1 35	1 50
Harpenden ...	2 5	2 15 LE. SO.
St. Albans ...	2 30	......
Harpenden ...	......	2 33 S.X.
Redbourn ...	2 48	3 13 S.X.
Godwin's Halt...	3 25	3 50 S.X.
Hemel Hempsted	3 57	4 18 S.X.
Heath Park ...	4 25	4 30 S.X.
Gas Works Sdgs.	4 37	5 5 S.X.
Hemel Hempsted	5 15	6 5 S.X.
Redbourn ...	6 30	6 47 S.X.
Harpenden ...	7 12	7 27 S.X.
St. Albans ...	7 40	......

Detach, attach or Shunt at Godwin Sdgs. or Station Yards as required.

Work as required.

St. Albans	8 30 L.E. S.X.
St. Albans Loco. Shed	......

a 30 cwt crane and in the yard was a weighbridge and weighbridge hut, where the key to the level crossing gates hung. LMS instructions later decreed that these gates must always be kept open for public access.

To return to the gas company and its wagons, they had for some time been using a wagon, No. 174, owned by a Board member, Mr Horsley, and in November 1882 they paid him £30 for it, and numbered it No. 3. However, in May 1899, all three of the gas company's wagons were condemned by the Midland, at which time they were put up for sale. S. Claye (wagonmakers) offered £5 for each wagon, on condition the company bought new 8 ton wagons from them at £59 each. Since the gas company declined to purchase, and no-one else appeared to want them, they gave consideration to breaking them up, but at the last minute the Midland Railway Company offered £6 10s. for No. 3, and two months later paid the same price for Nos. 1 and 2. More wagons had been purchased by the gas company in 1893.

By 1902 the goods area by Cotterells Road was arousing strong disapproval from certain official bodies in Hemel Hempstead and the whole performance of the Midland branch left much to be desired by the community. The Secretary of the Ratepayers' Association was asked to write to the proprietors of the *A.B.C. Guide*, pointing out that Boxmoor was the main Hemel Hempstead station. During further discussion it was pointed out that the line to Cotterells and the gasworks was used by the Midland 'purely as a shunting ground' which 'has always been a sore point with the inhabitants'. Apparently, when complaints had been voiced about night shunting, a Midland official had come down, put his hands in his pockets and said 'Hemel Hempstead can do as it likes and we shall do as we like'!

Further, the Association considered that the Boxmoor Trustees, in selling the land for a railway, had 'committed a crime' and that 'a certain number of passenger trains should have been insisted upon'. A railway line running in front of Cotterells Road houses 'upset a picturesque view, was most unsightly and would certainly not be allowed today', they said.

The problem rumbled on, literally, until on 13th October the Council (as a result of further complaints regarding noisy midnight shunting at Cotterells) heard that the Midland had written saying they had requested their staff to exercise care in the future to prevent further cause for complaint. However, things got worse, not better, and the Council declared the line to be 'useless by day and a perfect nuisance by night'.

Meanwhile, the Midland had indeed gone its own way. It had sold another piece of surplus land to the gasworks, on 20th June, 1899, so that it could expand again. Later on other small alterations were made to the track in the vicinity of the gasworks, namely in May 1919 the catchpoint was moved closer to Heath Park and on the 6th November the gasworks siding was slewed over slightly.

A further Agreement, dated 2nd November, 1925, allowed the gas company to rent more land for coal storage, for which the LMS charged £2 pa, and when the gasworks needed a second siding, plans were drawn on 11th October, 1928 and approved by the Midland in June 1929. When built the two sidings had a capacity of 26 wagons. On 10th January, 1933 the gas company unsuccessfully applied for a siding connection to the main line at Boxmoor, which was only 21 chains beyond the end of the Hemel Hempstead branch.

Following the Grouping of 1923, the LMS looked at the whole question of goods traffic in the Boxmoor/Hemel Hempstead area and decided to concentrate its goods activities at Boxmoor station (on the old LNWR line), with the result that from October 1924 the former Midland Goods Depot at Hemel Hempstead station on the branch had practically ceased to exist. One van had been delivering from both stations but it was intended to use two from Boxmoor, to provide a better service. However, these arrangements did not affect whole-wagon deliveries, where consignees arranged their own carting - these could still use 'Midland' facilities, and small parcels for outlying districts (e.g. Leverstock Green) could still be collected from Hemel Hempstead station, although quicker delivery was envisaged through Boxmoor. Mr Groome, Boxmoor station master, had attended a Chamber of Commerce meeting to explain the new arrangements and no objections were raised.

So by 1930 the branch was only a shadow of its former self. The passenger service was drastically reduced, having been virtually replaced by a bus service, the goods department at Hemel Hempstead station had been superseded by Boxmoor - but the gasworks still needed coal. It is probably fair to say that the centre of railway activity, insofar as the branch was concerned, shifted to Cotterells Sidings, or Heath Park Depot, to give it its full name, and it is easy to understand local residents' dissatisfaction with the development.

The sidings were capable of holding a total of 61 wagons, with a maximum of 16 in the passing loop and various coal merchants were allowed to run their businesses from this depot. 'The Midland Wharf' was the address given for Messrs Dorrofield & Dell in 1891, but this could have referred to the yard at Hemel Hempstead. T.F. Poulter, though, was a coal merchant at Cotterells, as were Brentnall & Cleland and Woodman Bros (Coal & Corn Merchants), and these three companies worked private-owner coal wagons, carrying their own liveries.

However, it was gasworks traffic which brought most wagons to this section of line because these trains were officially required to reverse into Cotterells Sidings, where the engine could run round its wagons, using the passing loop, and then propel them into the gasworks sidings. On 14th June, 1958, 24 loaded wagons were seen entering the works.

Chapter Eleven

Staff

It is impossible to track down all the members of staff who, over the years, contributed to the running of this branch railway, but the following records and reminiscences give some idea of the work undertaken, the loyalty of the staff and the respect they earned from the communities they served. And their transgressions? Well, they go to show that railwaymen are only human!

Some members of staff worked for years without getting a mention anywhere, whilst another could make one comment and it reached the local press. Such was the case with the Chiltern Green station master, soon after the branch opened. He said that his job was 'now much more important, now I have an extra eight trains a day to deal with'. Perhaps he was seeking a little extra in his pay packet too.

Another man who saw the line open was William Renals, Hemel Hempstead's first station master. He remained there for 10 years, until he was forced to retire early due to ill health, after 30 years as a railwayman. He died four years later, leaving a widow and five children. It is not known whether Joseph Hartley succeeded Mr Renals, but he was certainly occupying the post of station master around 1894. In 1898 Mr R. Foskett took over. He was later described as 'the genial station master', a point proved in September 1903 when season ticket holders and a few others presented him with an envelope containing £6 9s. 6d., as a token of thanks for his efforts towards the 'vastly improved' train service on the branch. In December 1904 he was promoted to Tottenham station.

He was succeeded by Henry Cross, who, after a period abroad, had joined the Midland Railway and served as station master in four towns, then as assistant traffic inspector at Stockport. He worked at Hemel Hempstead for the best part of 16 years and his varied railway experience had proved invaluable when the Midland and LNWR made arrangements for the pooling of traffic.

In February 1920 Mr Cross was found to have an inoperable growth and, after four months in bed, he died on 6th June - just five weeks before his 60th birthday (the age at which he could qualify for a railway pension). His funeral was held at St Paul's Church, where he had been both Sunday School Superintendent and a sidesman. Revd Boswall paid tribute to a 'man in a thousand' who had 'made hosts of friends and no enemies'. Mr Cross left a widow, three sons and a grand-daughter and railway colleagues, at their own request, carried the coffin at the Borough Cemetery. His successor, Mr R.A. Gill, was appointed the following October (promoted from Henlow station) and he was still there in 1924.

At midnight on 26th September, 1919 a rail strike began which was observed by almost all the Midland staff at Hemel Hempstead. Thus, all branch trains were suspended, but a few drivers started back on 3rd October, when a reduced service was run. The head drayman looked after the horses in the Hemel Hempstead stables, whilst two other draymen were sent to work elsewhere, and the clerks (who were also not on strike) handled a variety of jobs until the strike officially ended on 5th October.

In September 1924 William Sear, a well-respected Hempsteadian and long-serving Midland Railway employee, died. Another well-known figure in the town, Jonah Chappell, who had delivered parcels for the Midland for 33 years, retired in 1929.

Turning to Redbourn station, Mr G.W. Ashley may have been the first station master, as he spent about 25 years there. It is not certain whether he was promoted or retired on 29th January, 1904, but on 19th February at the Bull Hotel, Redbourn, Mr R.C. Peake, JP made a speech and presented Mr Ashley with a 'handsome gold watch and chain', subscribed for by the gentlemen of the village.

Mr Oliver Rignall came from Piddington & Horton station to be Redbourn's next station master, but his time there was saddened by the death of his 4-year-old son, on 7th November, 1908, from diphtheria. At the time, his wife was also seriously ill with the disease, but she eventually recovered. In 1910 Mr Rignall was promoted to Denby, in Derbyshire, at which time it was announced that he would not be replaced. Instead the Harpenden station master would take charge of the two stations. However, a 'responsible clerk' from Harpenden would deputise at Redbourn and at the same time a direct telephone link was provided between the booking office at Redbourn and the station master's office at Harpenden.

Mr Howard was clerk at Redbourn in the late 1920s and told of railway employees there trying to grow rhubarb under the loading platform by the goods shed. They would inspect it daily to see if it had forced enough to harvest, but they had little success. He also remembered being busy on Saturday afternoons, issuing weekly season tickets (to Heath Park Halt) to about 30 or 40 girls who worked for Dickinson's, as there was never time on Monday mornings. When on duty at Bank Holidays, his wife joined him in the booking office for a picnic.

Delivery of goods from Redbourn station was undertaken by porters or private carters. John Morris was one such railwayman, delivery man. Another was 'Fisty' Fellowes, who owned his horse, but rented a flat 4-wheeled cart from the railway and was paid on tonnage delivered. Among his jobs was the emptying of the station cesspit, but delivering goods was his main occupation. However, he sometimes turned up at the station having first consumed a quantity of liquor, whereupon the station staff would refuse him work, put him on his dray, pat the horse and it would take him home!

Information on platelayers is very hard to find and usually only comes to light when one was involved in some unfortunate circumstance. Such was the case with George Bunnage, of Kinsbourne Green (Harpenden). He had worked for the Midland Railway for 30 years, when on Tuesday 5th May, 1908 he had left home, as usual, at 5.30 am and was seen entering the platelayers' hut by Old Bell Bridge (A1081) at about 8 am. A few minutes later he was discovered in a collapsed condition by fellow workmen, Joseph Starkin and George Deacon. An inquest at Kinsbourne Green School, on 7th May, heard evidence which indicated the 69-year-old suffered a heart attack.

Another unfortunate happening, involving members of staff, occurred on Monday afternoon of 25th October, 1909 at Godwin's Siding. John Hull, a Midland Railway labourer, was helping to move a truck which had been damaged in a collision during shunting the previous Saturday night. Whilst using a crowbar on the wheel, a buffer, which had become wedged in the accident, suddenly sprang out, striking his head and catapulting him against the siding rails. Hull was taken, unconscious, to West Herts Hospital with several fractures of the skull. There he was operated on and by the following Friday he had regained consciousness. The authors have, in their collection, a Midland Railway Ambulance silver medal which was awarded to George Stripp (a railway employee) for 'First Aid Rendered at Hemel Hempstead October 25 1909', which would appear to be related to the above accident.

Engine drivers for branch trains were based at St Albans shed, and later at Cricklewood, but guards and shunters were taken from Harpenden, where they worked as porters and shunters in between branch working. Arthur Kingham was a passenger guard for 50 years, until he retired in 1946 and Robert Dunham was a guard for 37 years, until he also retired in January 1939. He was the guard on the train used for the film 'The Love Race', part of which was shot on the line.

During the latter days of BR goods working, four shunters and guards carried out branch duties, namely Harold Burns, Cuthbert Goldhawk, Percy Large and Sammy Newbold. The latter was well known for his pet phrase 'It's a dry old job this, boy!' - and to prove it, his train would often be found, hissing gently to itself, whilst its crew would be found either in the 'Saracen's Head', Redbourn, the Midland Hotel at Hemel Hempstead or the Heath Park Hotel at the end of the line!

The countryside around Redbourn put the meat on the table for some train crews. They would stop their train, set a snare and proceed on their journey, checking it the next day to either re-set it or remove a rabbit. Some crew members were accurate shots, again felling rabbits with small pieces of coal from the tender. Chickens, too, had a tendency to disappear if they strayed near the line, and some railwaymen knew where to look for new-laid eggs. Crews also swapped coal from the tender for apples from an adjoining orchard.

Some train crews tried to be entrepreneurial. There were several fields of Christmas trees beside the line and in the festive season unofficial 'orders' were taken for friends and family. Suitable trees were dug up in the dark, transported in the guards van and delivered to their 'customers' with the roots still wet. Many of these trees were potted up so quickly that they continued to grow!

Whilst some members of staff lived close to the line, others had to travel some distance to get to work. One shunter came from Cricklewood by Green Line bus, whilst another relied on his faithful motorbike. Some members of staff loyally did their job and passed on to other work or different areas without leaving anything to remember them by. Others, however, are clearly remembered for the colourful characters they were - such as the clog-wearing shunter who smoked shag twist in a mini-pipe and did his courting in the porters' room at Redbourn after the last train had left.

Turning lastly to signalmen, Harpenden Junction signal box, standing at the

Harpenden Junction signal box. Signalman Woodward is seen at the window of the signal box, while platelayer Mr Andrews is seen on the track, September 1937.   *G. Woodward*

entrance to the branch, was worked by many long-serving railwaymen. George Firbank retired in 1935 and the author's grandfather, John Woodward, retired on 31st March, 1939, having spent 37 years on the railway, first with the Midland Railway and then the LMS. It was he who made a stool for Brian Moules, the booking boy at the Junction, to stand on in order to be able to reach the train register desk.

William Pepper started as a porter at Redbourn in 1914, and progressed to become a signalman at the Junction in 1926. He retired in January 1959. Alfred Morgan worked the old Junction signal box and the new one, until he too retired in 1978. The night of 11th June, 1966 was one well-remembered by signalman, Jimmy King. There was a storm raging and at 1.30 am while he was pulling levers, the signal box was struck by lightning. He was thrown against the wall, but after treatment, completed his shift.

The last regular signalman was John Wood, who left the Junction on 16th September, 1978. While he was on duty he always kept a supply of biscuits for a squirrel and her babies, who made their presence known by tapping on the window of the signal box. There was also a small deer which lived on the banks of the branch, near the Junction, and this would allow John to approach and get very close. It was still there several years later.

Signalman Bill Pepper has just handed the staff to the crew of '3F' No. 43245 heading the LCGB's 'Nickey Special' on 11th May, 1957.   *A. Turner*

Chapter Twelve

Mishaps and Happenings

The Hemel Hempstead branch may only have been short in terms of miles, but it was not short of incidents. An early mishap occurred on 2nd June, 1884 when an engine boiler burst, soon after bringing a goods train into Godwin's Siding. No-one was hurt but delays occurred until a relief engine arrived from St Albans. Godwin's was the scene of another problem, on 10th January, 1885, when a luggage train from Hemel Hempstead derailed on the points and partially blocked the line. Mr Renals, Hemel Hempstead station master, telephoned London for a breakdown crane and also conveyed a message to passengers waiting at Chiltern Green that there would be a two-hour delay. However, an engine and coach were dispatched from Luton to pick up these people, and proceeded as far as Godwin's Siding, pulling up a few feet from the derailed train. It was raining, and daylight was fading, as passengers discussed among themselves what they should do next. To make matters worse, a porter arrived from Hemel Hempstead to collect their tickets 'as a precautionary measure'! He informed them there would be a delay and so they set off on foot along the line, some carrying babies.

Another derailment occurred at 12.45 pm on 9th September, 1890. A freight train (three full coal wagons, one of stone and a guard's van) passed Godwin's and, as usual, the driver shut off steam to descend the incline to Hemel Hempstead. Part-way down a steam valve failed and the train gathered speed. It ran through the station at about 35 mph, into the siding near Crescent Road, finally smashing into the massive buffer stop built of sleepers and earth. The engine tipped over into a garden but the driver and fireman escaped with no more than a severe shaking and the guard, who had jumped off, received only a bruised hand. The wagons were severely damaged, but the engine suffered little. However, it took 18 men and a breakdown crane from Childs Hill two days to re-rail the engine, watched by a large crowd. It was taken to St Albans for inspection, prior to going to Derby for repair.

The following three incidents all involved trains being driven by Henry Leadbetter - who must have started to wonder what else fate had in store for him! The first misfortune happened on 27th March, 1897 and concerned the turntable at Hemel Hempstead (ordered by Col Yolland before allowing the line to open). At 5.45 pm Leadbetter drove his engine out of the shed to prepare for the 6 pm train to Harpenden but it fell through the turntable and listed to one side, 1½ feet below ground level. Driver Leadbetter, fireman Bird and guard Dilley took a trap to Harpenden, where they obtained another engine to rescue the stranded coaches.

The following Sunday a breakdown gang arrived at 8.30 am to attend to the stricken engine, watched by several hundred people, but at 12 noon the engine was still in the pit. Inspector Garrett of the Locomotive Department contacted Mr Hart of the Compass Inn, High Street, and he laid on a meal for the men at 1 pm. By 4.15 pm the engine had been raised to ground level and another engine was brought 'within a safe distance and a stout rope attached'. Slowly the crippled engine was hauled back to firm track, as a hearty cheer rose from the crowd at 4.35 pm. The breakdown train left at 6 pm leaving behind it a completely smashed turntable, which was never rebuilt, but the brickwork was still evident after the branch closed.

Two months later, on Friday 28th May, a 3-year-old boy and his 17-month-old brother were at Woodend (between Redbourn and Godwin's) to see the 9.15 am train from Hemel Hempstead. For some reason they decided to cross the track in front of the train. The older boy got across in time, but the toddler was struck by the engine's coupling chain. Driver Leadbetter stopped his train and ran back to find the child crying. He took him home and a doctor was called, but luckily the child suffered only slight concussion.

Not so fortunate was the victim of Leadbetter's third incident. On 7th September, 1905 he worked a special goods train to Hemel Hempstead, which passed through Redbourn at 11 am. He neither saw, nor felt, anything unusual, but on his return at 11.45 am he saw five men at Connor's Crossing, just west of Redbourn station, and stopped when he saw 'a man laying there dead'. The deceased was identified as Edward Lee, a rat catcher known locally as 'The Warrener'. Evidence was given that the man's injuries were consistent with having been struck by a train, but the Coroner was puzzled as to why the man, aged 85, was hit, since he had good vision and hearing. Mr Leadbetter said no whistle had been sounded on the approach to the crossing, as this was only done if someone was seen there. The Coroner stated he would report to the Board of Trade suggesting that as 100 people a day used the crossing, a footbridge should be erected by the railway company - but if he did, nothing came of the suggestion.

Two other incidents occurred in 1897. In May, during shunting at Hemel Hempstead, a guard overbalanced and fell from his train, landing on his head and suffering severe bruising, and in October a Hemel Hempstead train burst a boiler tube at Redbourn. A messenger was dispatched to Harpenden, where a replacement engine was summoned from St Albans, which arrived an hour later.

Midland staff found themselves with a more serious situation, though, on 3rd November, 1901. The 1.10 am train was climbing up towards Roundwood (known to railwaymen as Bell Bank, after the 'Old Bell' public house nearby), when the crew noticed a body beside the track. Upon investigation they found David Gee, a 48-year-old from Guildford. A porter who happened to be on the train stayed with Gee while the train went to Redbourn, where the engine was run round, and the train brought back 'to a spot 315 yards west of Luton Road bridge'. Deciding not to move the injured man, they left to obtain further help from Harpenden, and returned later with Mr Horne, the station master. Gee was then put on the train but died shortly afterwards.

Driver Edward Lawrence told the Coroner how he had taken the earlier luggage train along the line at 10.55 pm from Harpenden and returned about 12.35 am, but he had noticed nothing unusual. It became evident that Gee had been run over by this train, and the Coroner questioned the crew's handling of the affair, but accepted they were doing their best in not wanting to move the injured man without advice, even though it was a cold foggy night.

Two incidents happened within a few weeks in 1904, the first on Easter

Monday, 4th April, when the early morning train to Harpenden failed between Hemel Hempstead and Redbourn, causing a two-hour delay in the passenger service while another engine was found, and during shunting at Harpenden on 28th April a carriage and goods van of the Hemel Hempstead train became derailed. A porter, who had been standing on the footboard, managed to jump clear. The derailment caused only slight delays to main line trains and the Cricklewood breakdown gang put matters right during the afternoon.

Being a country route, it was only to be expected that animals would occasionally 'trespass' on the railway - and suffer the consequences. On the evening of 26th September, 1891, 10 sheep, owned by Mr Waterton of Revel End Farm, Redbourn, were run down by a passenger train and on 16th August, 1901 a stray pony was killed by a train at Redbourn. During a hunt on 16th January, 1909, the Hertfordshire Hounds also ventured along this stretch of line. While some of the huntsmen tried to remove the dogs others waved their hats to indicate their presence to the driver of a train which had suddenly appeared, but he took no notice and one dog was run over.

At the other end of the branch, on 27th August, 1903, a young lady, who was riding a hired bicycle down Charles Street hill, lost control of her machine and careered into the iron fencing of the Goods Depot in Cotterells Road. She received a terribly gashed face and badly damaged the cycle.

Extremes of weather created problems for most railways, and the branch suffered small upsets from time to time. Winter weather delayed a Hemel Hempstead train on Boxing Day 1906, when snow blocked the wheels of the engine, and two months later a gale blew down brickwork from Paradise Bridge, near Marlowes, Hemel Hempstead, whereupon police called up Mr Cross, the station master, to warn the driver of the midnight goods train from Cotterells Siding. In May 1908 heavy rain resulted in Harpenden Lane, Redbourn being entirely flooded in the vicinity of the railway bridge and in November 1928 the line was closed while a tree which had been blown down in a gale, was removed from Godwin's Halt.

Another white Christmas was recalled by an ex-Redbourn booking clerk, who closed the station after the last train on Christmas Eve and went to Radlett for Christmas Day. He was due to re-open Redbourn Station at 6.30 am, on Boxing Day, but deep snow hampered his journey back. Eventually he reached Harpenden station, where he was told to walk to the Junction and join a light engine which was going to attempt to get through the drifts on the branch. It eventually succeeded, and having reached Redbourn the clerk lit a fire and dried himself out and not one passenger was seen there all day!

Another accident happened in April 1910. The 7.58 am from Harpenden had just left Redbourn when it struck a horse and cart standing on Connor's Crossing. The cart was smashed and the horse was carried 30 yards along the track. The animal belonged to Mr G.G. Webb of Redbourn, and was employed on scavenging work for the District Council. The man in charge, being a new hand to the job, was unaware of train times, and was locking the gate when the accident happened. Observations were made that as the crossing was visible from the station, and the train was travelling slowly, the driver could have pulled up in time to avoid a collision.

In July 1910 the Boxmoor Trustees had a problem. Evidently polluted water was running down from the gasworks site, alongside the branch as far as the A41 bridge, and down the embankment into drainage ditches beside the road. It then ran in a ditch, over the Moor and into the river. Trustees observed that the chemicals it carried were killing the grass on either side and decreed that 'It must stop!'. The problem was solved between the Boxmoor Trust and the Midland Railway (but no mention of action from the gasworks authorities) by an Agreement dated 10th October, 1911, whereby a catch pit and drain would be built on railway land by the bridge, with a drain laid alongside the road, for which the Trust would pay 2s. 6d. a year for as long as it was needed. However, the Council were not best pleased at having polluted water in their sewers!

In the same area, in the early hours of Saturday 9th December, 1911 three wagons derailed on points at Heath Park. The train pulled up quickly so no damage resulted, and as the wagons were soon re-railed little delay was caused. During that year there was much talk of a scheme to link the branch to the LNWR main line at Boxmoor, and a public petition was later raised in support of the idea. Nothing came of it, but on 26th June, 1915, six wagons ran away from Hemel Hempstead station and 'made good speed' as far as the gasworks, where they came to rest. Those who had long advocated the scheme to link the two lines saw this 'as a good omen'!

From 1st January, 1883 the Midland Railway Company provided a delivery service for Hemel Hempstead, using its own horses and drays, but not without incident. On 5th May, 1897, in the High Street, drayman James Dyer was pitched into the road and nearly run over when an axle pin dropped out which disconnected the shafts.

The early 1900s saw an increase in the number and variety of road vehicles and concern was voiced in Hemel Hempstead about youngsters taking risks through chasing and dodging moving vehicles. One of these incidents happened on 1st June, 1901 in Marlowes, when a youth, who had been hanging on a Midland trolley, was observed by the carman. To avoid being caught, the youth jumped off and immediately collided with Councillor Fisher's bicycle 'causing a nasty spill', but no serious injuries.

Fortunately no-one was hurt on 20th November, 1903 when a 'powerful motor-car' ran into a stationary dray in Hemel Hempstead High Street. In fact it wedged under the dray, between the front and back wheels. The horse attempted to bolt, but was 'pluckily stopped by PC Hunt'. Seven or eight men lifted the trolley sufficiently for the car to be extricated and, although its lamps and front were damaged, it continued on its journey.

In March/April 1904 an outbreak of influenza hit the Midland stables at Hemel Hempstead. Four horses suffered and a valuable roan died a few weeks later. The LNWR also lost a dray horse during this period, when it died in harness, as a result of heart failure, on the bridge above the Midland station.

Later that year a dray horse bolted out of the goods yard and the attached dray was badly damaged when it collided with a wall, and just before Christmas 1914 a Midland horse slipped and fell through a High Street shop window, receiving a cut neck. Only prompt action by a vet saved its life.

Whilst on the subject of horses, in December 1908 a Christmas reveller tried to drive his pony and chaise through the doors of Hemel Hempstead station booking hall and, on 4th March, 1912, a horse, frightened by a train at Redbourn, bolted and collided with a gate, overturning the cart. It is also on record that one of Brentnall & Cleland's horses bolted when leaving Cotterells Depot with a 15 cwt load of coal, nearly colliding with a loaded hearse, before it was pulled up.

The branch was used on more than one occasion as a getaway route by thieves. In August 1888, having stolen tools from Thorogood's shop in Redbourn, the culprits travelled by train to Harpenden. There, a porter named Ward noticed the two tool baskets they carried, and two weeks later he went to Clerkenwell to identify the men.

On 22nd January, 1890 a Court heard about William Kilsby and Alfred Spicer. The former had stayed with the latter and stole from him a £5 note, a silver watch and half a sovereign. Acting on information received, Police Sergeant Frogley had gone to Hemel Hempstead station, where he found Kilsby about to depart on the 5.55 pm train. 'I want you', he said, and told him the charge, whereupon Kilsby produced the note, the watch and a ticket to St Pancras, plus 10s. 11½d., having bought his ticket with the half sovereign. He was committed for trial on this charge, having the previous year served a three-month prison sentence for stealing a horse.

In May 1928 two burglars were arrested at Hemel Hempstead station, as they alighted from a train, after a tip-off from Harpenden police and in July 1933 a prisoner, who had escaped from St Albans police station, was found dead on the branch at Redbourn.

Even railway premises were not immune from crime. A serious theft occurred within Hemel Hempstead Goods Department on or around 15th December, 1920, when a dress basket belonging to a Miss Docherty was ransacked. She was moving house and had packed the basket with handbags, blouses, new underwear, gloves, stockings, books (including one of newspaper cuttings), private letters and jewellery (including items containing diamonds, rubies and sapphires). By 5th February, 1921 nothing had been recovered, although the police announced they 'had the matter in hand'. Miss Docherty is understood to have said that the items had 'no mean intrinsic value, just sentimental value, which no amount of compensation can adequately recompense'.

Redbourn station, too, was the scene of a burglary in December 1927, when two new oil stoves, some parcels and the contents of the chocolate slot machine were taken, plus 3s. 9d. in cash. In August 1957 three men were arrested after being chased along the branch by police. They were finally caught near Hemel Hempstead station, around midnight.

Children, too, appeared in Court as a result of incidents connected with the line. One such session was held on 28th June, 1916, when Eric Pettitt, aged 12, Maurice Pettitt, 9, and John Wells, 9, pleaded guilty to 'doing damage to Midland Railway property at Hemel Hempstead station'. Mr Cross, station master, had been walking across the bridge at 9.15 pm when he looked down and saw the boys running about on the station platform. He recognised Eric Pettitt, but the boys ran away as he approached. On examination, he discovered the station entrance door glass smashed, together with the glass fronts of three automatic vending machines. The wooden office door was also damaged but he found the only missing items were 22 packets of chocolate from the machines.

By coincidence, Mr Cross met up with Pettitt later in the evening and made a citizen's arrest. At the police station, Pettitt at first gave a false name, but then he admitted the offence and named his accomplices. They were brought in, and between them they produced some of the chocolate bars. In Court it was said that the damage was estimated by the railway company at 30s. and the boys were bound over to be of good behaviour for three years, and given a good talking to by the Court Chairman. Their fathers stated in Court that they had given their boys 'good thrashings', but nevertheless Walter Pettitt was ordered to pay 16s. 8d. costs and Mr Wells 8s. 4d. in respect of their sons' transgressions.

Four more boys were taken to Court on 4th July for trespassing on the railway at Highfield footbridge. The fire buckets, which hung on the bridge had been damaged and the local constable put two and two together when he witnessed the boys attempting to damage some railings. It was pointed out during the case that the 'railway was like a promenade up there on a Sunday - it being lovely countryside'. The evidence to the fire buckets being somewhat vague, the Chairman concentrated his remarks to the general public, insisting that these Sunday afternoon strolls along the railway had got to stop.

It seems the same problem existed at the Harpenden end of the line also. On 9th January, 1948 five boys, aged between 11 and 13, were discovered in a platelayers' hut near the A6 (A1081) bridge. They had a roaring fire going, on which they had cooked bread and potatoes (having equipped themselves with the necessary cooking utensils). At the Court hearing in March they said they were only sheltering from the rain, and their parents could see no problem in them being there, 'as many people used the railway as a walkway'.

Another path the public were not supposed to use ran along the inside of the railway fence between Hemel Hempstead station and Paradise, and this was sometimes used as a short cut to reach the station. On 12th February, 1926 the body of Arthur Godwin was found on this path and it transpired that he had

Deeley '3F' No. 43782 has become derailed at Hemel Hempstead station, Johnson '3F' No. 43565 has been coupled to it in readiness for pulling the engine back on the road, June 1955.   *A.D. Edwards*

probably felt unwell at his draper's shop in Marlowes and left early to catch the 4.55 pm train (instead of his usual 6.40 pm train) to Harpenden, where he lived. To reach the footpath he had had to climb over a 5 ft 3 in. 5-bar fence which the railway authorities had built to keep people out, and possibly this effort had brought about his collapse.

A story with a happier ending relates to an excursion which was organised to Southend-on-Sea on Wednesday 11th July, 1923. Provision had to be made for a large party joining at Redbourn, thus a rather larger train than normal was run through to Hemel Hempstead, where a few excursionists got aboard, as well as some workmen who were bound for Luton.

It was a damp, misty morning, but 'full of hope', the train steamed out of the station, only to find that because of the excess weight and state of the rails, it could not climb the immediate gradient. To resolve the matter officials, workmen and passengers disembarked and threw sand and dirt on the rails for the wheels to obtain a grip. After some unsuccessful attempts, the train managed to reach Redbourn, where a party of several hundred school children boarded - and again the train refused the gradient. To overcome the problem someone walked back to Redbourn station and a telephone message resulted in a fresh engine being sent from Harpenden to render assistance, after which all experienced 'a fine trip'. The following week a second trip was scheduled, and the railway authorities went to great lengths to assure the public 'these troubles will not recur' - and they didn't!

The line was, in fact, well used by school children over the years travelling either to Harpenden, St Albans or Hemel Hempstead. Soon after World War I one young lad, George Grigs, was a pupil at a St Albans school, when he was invited to tea with a pal in Harpenden. On his way home to Hemel Hempstead his curiosity with the railway scene got the better of him and he did the unforgivable - he leaned out of the carriage window. The next he remembers is being on the track, feeling sore and alone. His cries for help were heard by some farmworkers at Woodend, who found him in the dark and rescued him (remarkably he was not badly injured in his fall). A lady passenger had missed his presence in the carriage, but even though she shouted out of the window to try to attract the driver of the train, she could not be heard over the noise of the engine, and it was only when the train arrived at Godwin's Halt that anyone became aware of the situation.

Two other stories are told by a Redbourn resident, who also used the branch to travel to school, this time in Hemel Hempstead. The first referred to a Harpenden girl, nicknamed 'Pudding', who decided all the boys should be able to dance properly by the time the school dance was held, and accordingly took along a gramophone and gave dancing lessons in the guard's van. His second recollection was of the tremendous vibration which ran through the train after it collided with, and killed, a cow at Beaumont's Halt.

Another local resident, once an employee of Rothamsted Experimental Station, recalls how sheep, too, would occasionally stray onto the line through an unsecured gate. 'During World War II we wanted some meat for a Harvest Supper, to go with the farm-produced potatoes and turnips', she recalls, 'but meat was rationed and the sale of animals for slaughter was restricted'.

However, a suitable animal coincidentally 'became available' - appearing in the monthly returns from Rothamsted Farm as 'Killed on the Railway'! The hand of providence?

The branch underbridges were often in the news for one reason or another. The large bridge over the Luton Road (A1081) at Harpenden caused concern because of a narrow tapering pavement, and the one which crossed Harpenden Lane at Redbourn was quite regularly struck by lorries, or had lorries wedged under it. However, at 3 pm on Sunday 6th November, 1910 the police were more concerned with the cardplaying and gaming they found going on beneath it, a discovery which led Abel King, Harry King, George Halsey and Bertie Fox to St Albans County Sessions. However, only Harry King and Bertie Fox turned up and fines were fixed between 2s. 6d. and 5s. on the four men, based on their appearance or non-appearance and previous convictions.

Other bridges in trouble were the A5 bridge at Redbourn, where in June 1930 an electric generator, *en route* from Coventry to Southend by road, got jammed for four hours, and the London Road (A41) at Boxmoor which suffered damage when it was hit by a lorry carrying concrete beams on Monday 9th February, 1953 - just one of the many knocks it received.

It is rare for cars to be involved in railway incidents but in March 1954 a car chase ended in Townsend Lane, Harpenden, when police arrested post office raiders after they had gained access to the branch, via a crossing, and made a vain attempt at driving their car along the track.

At the same place, during the early hours of Saturday 15th December, 1956, another driver had a lucky escape. He had been driving along unfamiliar roads in Harpenden, after visiting friends, and, having taken a wrong turn, found himself on the Townsend Lane crossing. Realising his error, he tried to reverse, but his car wheels had stuck. He got out to investigate and when he got back in he could not start the vehicle. He was still trying to start the car when he heard a train approaching. It hit his car square-on, pushing it 75 yards along the track. The driver suffered shock and bruises and afterwards called the experience 'a bit of a nightmare'!

Yes - the branch had perhaps more than its fair share of accidents and incidents, but on the whole it was just a quiet country line, and because of this it was considered an ideal film location on several occasions. In 1931 Redbourn appeared in the musical comedy 'The Love Race', starring Stanley Lupino and Jack Hobbs, and just before nationalisation the LMS produced an instructional film on the subject of 'Locomotive Firing', part of which was filmed on the branch. The film crew travelled on a flat wagon sandwiched between engine No. 4777 and the tender (which made life difficult for the fireman) and at times the train reached 15 mph (which made life difficult for the film crew!).

Another film crew visited the branch around 1964 to record an episode of 'The Baron', at Redbourn. An '08' diesel shunter from St Albans was hired out with its driver and guard, and after partaking of the freely available refreshment the guard commented that it was probably his best day on the railway.

During the freight-only days of the branch little maintenance was carried out and this resulted in several derailments, but not all were caused by the state of the track. The following accident would not have happened if the train staff

Luton Road bridge, Harpenden, suitably decorated for the Festival of Britain, May 1951.

Authors' Collection

had adopted the correct procedure for shunting wagons into the gas works at Boxmoor. Instead they had devised a quicker method, whereby the train would stop short of the points into Cotterells, the guard would then apply his brake whilst the engine was uncoupled and run forward to Heath Park. Cotterells Siding points were then reversed and the engine ran in. Once clear of the points, they were changed back, the engine whistled and the guard released his brake, allowing the wagons to free-wheel past the points, with the engine then coming out to propel them to the works.

Such was the intention on 13th September, 1949, but with part of the procedure completed the driver noticed children playing on the line and he warned them off by blowing his whistle. The guard took this as his signal to set the wagons free, but the engine had not in fact cleared the points, resulting in a collision. Several wagons were derailed and the Cricklewood crane had to be called in.

Derailments at Hemel Hempstead in its later years were quite common, particularly on the three-way points in the goods yard. Engine No. 43888 came off the track on 12th April, 1954 and when No. 44259 derailed a sister engine re-railed it. Engine No. 43782 went through some points as they were being moved, in June 1955, and No. 43565 was used to pull it back on again, before both running 'light engine' to Harpenden. On another occasion the breakdown crane was being remarshalled ready to return to Cricklewood, having re-railed an engine, when the crane itself left the track at the same spot. Story has it that after one derailment an observer was told that overtime could always be arranged simply by derailing a wagon or front wheels of an engine! However, it was the rotten state of the sleepers, which allowed the track to spread, that accounted for engine No. 43119 being completely derailed at Redbourn on 26th June, 1958.

Another problem which probably arose due to lack of maintenance, was the inability of the signalman to reverse the points at Harpenden Junction after branch trains had rejoined the main line. This seizing-up meant that the down fast line was blocked until a crew turned up to release the points - and they were needed more than once!

So the branch had its mishaps and its amusing moments, but most of the time it just got on with its work, and looked like any other country branch line. Its embankments were originally kept clear of foliage, but eventually they were taken over by brambles and hawthorn hedges, bluebells and other wild flowers. Children of the 1940s and 1950s crept up the line in the dark to look for glow-worms, whilst other local people would take strolls along the line on warm summer evenings to listen to the sweet song of the nightingales which inhabited the area.

Train drivers waved to excited children in the early days of Roundwood Junior School, just as they did to the farm workers on the Rothamsted Estate, and no doubt elsewhere, in much earlier days, and the sights and sounds of steam engines struggling to conquer the steep gradients would have changed little down the decades.

What did change, though, was social history and the A6 bridge at Harpenden came right up to date in May 1962 when someone daubed 'Ban the Bomb Now' slogans on both sides of it, only to be replaced two nights later by 'Keep Britain Great'!

The end of the line at Boxmoor gasworks, 6th July, 1958.   *Brian W. Leslie*

Demolition in progress at Marlowes viaduct in 1960.   *A.D. Edwards*

Chapter Thirteen

The End of 'The End of the Line'

The fate of the line between Hemel Hempstead station and the gasworks had hung in the balance for some time, but it was finally closed and taken over by Hemel Hempstead New Town Development Corporation on 31st August, 1959. To enable the gasworks to continue receiving coal, a connection was laid from Boxmoor Yard to the works, construction of which was well under way in March 1959, and it came into use when the other section closed. About 25 yards of track were retained beyond the A41 bridge, to serve as a backshunt to the works. However, this arrangement was shortlived, as the gasworks closed on 1st April, 1960; in fact the connection was disused for some time before this, as the gasworks used up existing coal stocks.

The point in Boxmoor Yard was clipped out of use, but remained until May 1972, when it was replaced by plain track. At that time the siding remained, but it was heavily overgrown. In 1962 a lorry jammed under the A41 bridge, resulting in the lifting of track and deck to release it.

Early in 1960 track was removed from Cotterells Depot - this was shown on the New Town Plan as being the site for Leighton Buzzard Road. Track was then taken up as far as Hemel Hempstead station and in May dragline cranes began to remove the embankments across the Moor, during which an estimated 76,000 cubic yards of soil was reinstated in the cutting behind Marlowes. Care was taken to damage as few trees as possible, so that the 'scar' would not show too much. Today the only remnants of the branch are a short length of embankment beside the A41, jutting brickwork where the line crossed the canal and two rows of trees behind the cricket pitch. The two road bridges at Heath Park were removed on Tuesday 31st May, 1960, the roads only closing for a short time. The previous January a lorry had struck one of these bridges and shed its load of aerosol cans.

Marlowes viaduct, which had taken so long to build, was demolished in a day. After closing Marlowes to road traffic, at 11 pm on Saturday 2nd July, 1960, holes were drilled in the crowns to help speed demolition. By 1 am on Sunday the first arch was down. The parapets were removed first and then a crane swung a heavy ball at the arches. All this was watched by a crowd of about 500 people and whenever the ball missed the brickwork shouts went up of 'Leave it alone' or 'Can we have our ball back, please?' The work was carried out by F.G. Fleming of Northchurch.

Hemel Hempstead station closed on 1st July, 1963, followed by Godwin's Sidings on 2nd March, 1964. Demolition work started immediately but stopped just west of Claydale Sidings, where a buffer stop was erected. The station site became a small housing development and the cutting from Queensway to Cupid Green was partially filled in and made into a pathway. Commercial buildings occupy the site where Godwin's Sidings stood. Development of the New Town included a vast industrial estate and this was sited near to the remaining section of the branch, in the hope that some firms would need private sidings. This did not materialise, but Hemelite at Claydale did still wish to use the line.

Since the track had barely been attended to since it was relaid between 1935 and 1938, rain had removed much of the gravel and ash ballast and by 1960 some of the sleepers were completely rotten. To rectify the situation every sixth or seventh sleeper was replaced with a good one. Strangely, these were brought from the Southern Region electric lines, some still bearing their third rail insulator brackets. A tamping machine was brought in but could not work, due to the lack of ballast. Following the relaying of Claydale Sidings, excess ballast was laid for some distance along the line, but it was never spread out.

Relaying of Claydale sidings in 1959.   *A.D. Edwards*

Chapter Fourteen

A New Lease of Life

Following World War II, Dennis Mortimer took over the brickworks at Cupid Green (Claydale) as a base for his road haulage business. Almost as a side-line he commenced production of clinker building blocks, using two German hand-operated machines. In 1958 Howards of Bedford took over the works and set about expanding production by installing new machinery in new buildings. In 1959 Railway & General Engineering of Nottingham were appointed to lift old, partly-buried sidings and relay with good used materials, at a cost of £10,000. A hydraulic tipper was installed on one siding, which raised each wagon to discharge its ash through an end door into a hopper between the rails, then on to a conveyor belt into the works.

Internal shunting was done by a 4-wheel Simplex locomotive, No. 9921/59. A new company - Hemelite (being a shortened version of Hemel Hempstead Lightweight Concrete Co. Ltd) was created and when coal traffic to Redbourn ceased on 6th June, 1964, Hemelite carried on as sole user of the branch.

When, in 1968, British Railways announced its intention to close the line, Hemelite's General Manager, Leslie Hammett, suggested a private lease and BR agreed. The line was declassified to siding status and an Agreement was made with Howards that they would be responsible for the cost of keeping the line open as from 1st February, 1968, until a decision had been made as to their application to work the line as a light railway.

However, opposition was voiced by Hertfordshire County Council, who feared a lack of proper maintenance, and wished to see the line closed so that some dangerous bridges could be removed. Notwithstanding this, Parliament approved a Bill in February 1969 for transfer of the line to Hemelite, and immediately the company ordered two Drewry diesel shunters from British Rail. D2207 arrived in March, marshalled behind a Type 2 locomotive, along with wagons of ash. To mark the Hemelite/BR boundary, two Limit of Shunt notices were erected about 30 yards west of the 25½ milepost at Harpenden.

Hemelite-bound ash trucks travelled down-country to Luton sidings. The company then informed BR of its daily requirements and the latter would haul that number of wagons to Harpenden. Since there were no sidings at Harpenden Junction, delivering and collecting branch line trucks proved extremely complicated, noisy and time-consuming - sometimes blocking the main fast lines for up to an hour. It was practical, therefore, to shunt at night when the main line was quiet, but this caused considerable annoyance to local residents.

The shunting procedure was as follows:

Loaded wagons would arrive at Harpenden Junction, pulled by the Luton 'trip' engine, usually a class '25'. The loaded wagons and back brake van would be left on the up fast line, just north of the junction points, while the uncoupled engine (joined to a second brake van) moved forward past the points, which were then changed behind them. This allowed the engine to reverse onto the down fast line for a short distance, where it

137

Wagons of ash, left by BR, being taken on to Claydale Sidings by the Hemelite-owned Drewry diesel-mechanical 0-6-0 shunter (ex-BR No. D2203) seen here at Ambrose Lane bridge, February 1969. *Authors' Collection*

deposited the brake van. The engine then moved forward clear of the branch points, which were then reversed, allowing the engine to run up and collect the empty wagons, which were subsequently placed on the down fast line with the brake van to anchor them.

The full wagons, less brake van, were then collected from the up fast line and pushed onto the branch, after which the engine would return to the down fast line to pick up the empty trucks with their brake van and cross back to the up fast line, where it was re-united with its back brake van. Once coupled, the train would proceed to Brent empty wagon sidings.

These movements were further complicated on one occasion when 60 empty wagons were involved, and again at 12.30 am on 6th August, 1971, when two wagons derailed while being propelled onto the branch, causing the main lines to be blocked for some time.

The second Drewry, No. D2203, arrived shortly after the takeover, being left at the back of a night delivery of 19 full wagons. The following morning an attempt was made to use the diesel to push the wagons to Hemelite, but the steep incline at Roundwood proved too much for the little engine. The matter was resolved by shunting in the usual way, a few wagons at a time. Both engines were painted bright red and carried large boards, hung from the hand-rails each side, with 'Hemelite' in large letters, and the company badge on the cabsides.

Two former steam engine firemen, Ken Allen and Jim Malyon, who had been displaced when St Albans shed closed, and who had worked over the line, were taken on as drivers for Hemelite. Norman Robbins was later recruited as a driver, being taught by the company and tested by BR.

A total of 16 new warning notices were erected at the crossings along the line, following an incident at Redbourn in June 1968 when the engine struck a tractor. Coincidentally, the engine hit the same tractor again in January 1971! A collision with one of Rothamsted's combine harvesters, which had stalled on a crossing, was averted when the train managed to stop just feet from the machine.

Lorries continued to get stuck under Harpenden Lane bridge at Redbourn, often moving it sideways. On 13th September, 1972 it was hit for the third time in two months, when a lorry carrying stainless steel sinks stuck under it. Lifting lugs, fitted after an earlier accident, allowed a crane to lift the bridge and release the lorry. On 6th November black and yellow dazzle stripes were painted on the bridge and low bridge signs erected, but they did not make much difference.

Early in 1972 both Drewrys were out of service and this resulted in the Simplex making its only journey to Harpenden Junction, to fetch a wagon of spare parts left by BR. In order to get ash moving again, Hemelite hired from BR, for a fortnight from 23rd May, 1972, a 350 hp '08' shunter, No. D4139, which arrived having travelled 'light engine' all the way from Preston!

As an experiment, Hemelite tried using hopper wagons, but these proved impractical during winter, when frozen ash blocked the bottom doors, making it difficult to unload.

Of the two Drewrys, No. D2203 proved to be the better engine and No. D2207 was moved to the end of the siding, where it was cannibalised for spare parts, but in 1973 it was sold to the North Yorkshire Moors Railway.

The company later saw the advantage of being able to shift wagons from

The Clayton at Claydale Sidings.   *Ken Allan*

Clayton No. D8568 stored in April 1976.   *Kevin Lane*

Harpenden Junction all in one go, rather than making several trips, and accordingly purchased Type 1 Clayton, No. D8568; a much more powerful engine. Ken Allen travelled to Glasgow, and accompanied a Polmadie driver on the 400 mile journey home with it. This served as his instruction course for working it, and conductors were picked up as necessary along the route. It arrived at Harpenden Junction at 11.09 pm on 1st September, 1972 and was put on the branch for the trip to Claydale. Meanwhile, a down passenger train was stopped to pick up the Polmadie driver and his conductor, to take them to Luton on the first leg of their journey home. It is said the driver was on duty for 36 hours.

The Clayton, however, did not enjoy a happy existence on the branch, as it failed to work properly almost from the beginning. Engineers spent many hours on it, even fitting new engines while it stood in a siding at Redbourn in 1975. When it did function, the noise and vibration drew complaints from residents all along the line. It was soon discarded and stored at the end of the line, where it was vandalised, and later put up for sale.

The engine made its last trip down the branch on Thursday 16th June, 1976, propelled by No. D2203, leaving Claydale at 9.30 am. On arrival at Harpenden Junction the keys were left with the signalman, ready for collection that night. It left for Cricklewood at 11.55 pm. On Monday, 20th June, it started its five day journey to its new owners, Ribblesdale Cement, at Clitheroe, behind the engine of a northbound freight train, and passed Harpenden Junction at 2.25 pm.

St Albans District Council placed a Compulsory Purchase Order on Redbourn Goods Yard in January 1974, but this was lifted after strong opposition from the company and local residents. The Council wanted 1.9 acres for an industrial site but the proposal was opposed on the grounds of increased traffic flow through the village.

With Hemelite firmly established, preservation societies sought permission to store rolling stock on the line, with a view to running, but they were all refused owing to the lack of siding space. However, the company did run special trains for enthusiasts, which consisted of two or three mineral wagons and an engine, although on one occasion a shortage of wagons meant that people had to travel on the engine (some in the cab, and the rest standing on the running plate, where they needed to keep a look-out for overhanging branches). The 'special' arranged for 12th May, 1973 was to have been hauled by the Clayton, but it was out of service, and in fact it never hauled a special train during its stay on the Branch. 'Specials' ran as follows:

10th May, 1969	Branch Line Society
17th October, 1970	Locomotive Club of Great Britain
7th August, 1971	Locomotive Club of Great Britain
12th May, 1973	Locomotive Club of Great Britain
17th May, 1975	Stour Valley Railway
14th June, 1975	Locomotive Club of Great Britain
19th June, 1976	Railway Correspondence & Travel Society
16th July, 1977	'Nickey' Centenary Special
9th June, 1979	Branch Line Society
each May	Weedkiller train

Simplex shunter (MR 9921) is seen at Claydale Brickworks, 8th April, 1976.   *Kevin Lane*

The centenary and original nameboards from the Drewry locomotive.   *Authors' Collection*

In 1977 BR heard about these special trains and banned further trips - considering loose-coupled wagons to be unsafe for passengers since there was no way of braking if a coupling broke. They were also concerned about the extra wear and tear on their wagons! The ruling was however, ignored when Branch Line Society members were transported by an engine and two coal wagons for the trip on 9th June, 1979.

Fate took a hand at 4.15 pm on 2nd March, 1977, when six wagons ran away from Hemelite's sidings. Once on the 1 in 57 gradient they picked up speed, until they smashed through the gates at Beaumont's Crossing. The leading wagon derailed, and before stopping some 100 yards further on, broke two sleepers and fifty chairs. Two new gates were quickly acquired and the wagons were retrieved by No. D2203 and the Simplex. As a result of this incident, BR insisted on rail clamps (scotch blocks) being fitted to the track on Three Cherry Trees Lane bridge, at the top of the incline. To warn of these clamps, notices and orange flashing warning lights were installed on either side, but they were vandalised soon after.

On 22nd April, 1977 No. D2203 delivered three wagons to the junction and then went back to base, after which its engine was removed and transported back to Drewry's works for a complete overhaul. Due to the fact that the line was becoming very overgrown and the 'Little Red Engine' had not been seen for several weeks, local people began to express regret that the line had closed just a few weeks before its centenary. However, No. D2203 returned on 4th June, refitted and repainted - but still red. Traffic resumed on the night of 15th June, when BR left 15 wagons on the branch. After the overhaul, which had cost £5,700, it was possible to track the progress of the engine by the trail of blue smoke it left behind!

On Saturday 16th July, 1977, the Harpenden to Hemel Hempstead Railway centenary was marked by events at both ends of the branch. Councillor Cyril Fowler, Chairman of Dacorum Council, joined 'friends of the line' for a short ceremony at 11 am outside the old Midland Hotel, opposite the site of Hemel Hempstead station. A commemorative plaque had been donated by the line's 'friends' and fixed to the outside wall of the hotel, where a 100-year old Danish tapestry of a railway engine was pulled back to unveil the plaque. As a security measure, the plaque was later moved inside the hotel, to its Railway Bar.

After the ceremony some people went on to Cupid Green, where Ken Allen got out No. D2203 and gave a footplate ride along the branch to eight enthusiasts, who then made their way to Harpenden Library, where the authors of this book had arranged a special exhibition of photographs, historical facts and relics of the branch, which aroused considerable interest in the town. During the day a visitor brought in and gave us a carriage key which had been used by her father when he was a member of the station staff at Hemel Hempstead.

Having celebrated its centenary, it was a case of 'back to work' for the branch, but it continued to experience incidents. On 25th August BR's engine went onto the branch as usual about midnight, but part of a fallen tree got tangled in the bogie. Guard Bill Kent tried to pull it out, and in doing so put his hand into a wasps' nest. Although badly stung, the shunting manoeuvre was completed. He received hospital treatment and was unable to work for a few days, but as he was the only guard who knew the branch at night, it was decided to cancel

Two views of Claydale sidings on 16th May, 1978   *Authors*

Friday night's trip. As the wagons were to remain on the branch over the weekend, the Area Manager came on Saturday to pin down all the brakes, bringing a brand new lever to do the job. Incidentally, the pest control man dealt with the wasps five days later.

A potentially dangerous situation arose in September 1977 when the shunting signal protecting the main line was propped up with a piece of wood, showing the 'clear' position. Fortunately, the signalman noticed the repeater in the signal box and the train crew checked it when they went over the line. Had it not been noticed the engine would have come round the corner to find the catchpoints open, thus derailing it.

Maintenance of the line was carried out in a very haphazard way, although the situation near Harpenden Junction was getting very bad with overhanging trees and undergrowth, about which the staff complained. When time allowed, the engine driver would stop to cut back greenery or replace missing keys, but at the beginning of November 1977 the A5 bridge at Redbourn was favoured with a coat of brown paint.

The beginning of the end came when BR announced its intention to electrify the London to Bedford main line, and by March 1978 BR had made it clear that the branch had no place in its plans. The problem was the facing point from the down main line at Harpenden Junction, once illustrated in an engineering journal as a bad situation for such a point. Studies were carried out to see if a route to Boxmoor Goods Yard was still available, and another idea was to reinstate the north curve at Harpenden, where the cutting remained, though overgrown with trees. These suggestions were virtually ruled out on cost.

1978 turned out to be something of a disaster year for the branch. By March it was common to find some of the shunting signals at Harpenden Junction without oil, because there were not enough staff to keep them topped up, and although the branch was shunted on the 7th, the crew refused to do so the following two nights until the lamps were relit. Harpenden Lane bridge at Redbourn was struck again by a lorry on 27th June, moving it out of line, and again on Monday, 31st October when a Pickford's furniture lorry moved it 2 ft out of line. Hemelite's engine was at Harpenden when it happened and had to remain at Roundwood Halt until the bridge was lifted back by a 20-wheel road crane on Thursday, 2nd November. By the end of 1978 there were no regular signalmen at Harpenden Junction, and as shifts were covered by reliefmen few night shifts were worked, which meant that ash supplies became most irregular.

In February 1979 BR announced that Harpenden Junction signal box was to close at the end of June and that the branch would be severed. Hemelite made efforts to increase traffic by asking a nearby scrap merchant to send their scrap away by rail, thus giving BR return loads, but this was only acceptable if a guaranteed 18 wagons a day were dispatched. The merchant was unable to meet such a figure, but for a short while Hemelite sent scrap away from its works by rail.

Forced to find an alternative, Hemelite sought permission from BR to unload its ash at Luton, or Leagrave and transfer it by road to Redbourn station site, where it had already built up a stockpile of ash, but it was told that there was no room at either place for such an operation. The final delivery of ash was shunted onto the branch on the night of Wednesday 27th June, 1979. The wagons were collected by

BR type 2 Bo-Bo No. 25 069 propels ash wagons onto the branch past Harpenden Junction signal box in April 1979. A rare photographic opportunity - this work was usually done at night.

R.E. Barnes

Locomotives Nos. 25 310 and 25 204 shunt wagons of ash on another rare daylight working at Harpenden Junction.

R.E. Barnes

Two views of the last journey on the branch from Claydale to Redbourn, 7th February, 1982.
(*Both*) *A. Wright*

Harpenden Junction showing the first rail sections on the branch removed, 18th October, 1979. Colour light signals can be seen alongside semaphore signals. *Authors*

Work on the removal of the point for the Hemel branch at Harpenden Junction, 21st March, 1980. *Authors*

Demolition of Harpenden Junction signal box is in progress in this view of 17th February, 1981. Note that overhead wires are now in place on the main line. *Authors*

Hemelite during the next day, the empty wagons being returned on Friday, 29th.

Still not beaten, Hemelite purchased four 21-ton hopper wagons from Cohen's at Kettering. These came by road to Redbourn and were put on the line with the intention of moving the ash stocks there, thus keeping part of the line in use until arrangements could hopefully be made with BR for normal traffic to recommence. These wagons were in a sorry state, being rusty and holed. Two had lost their plates, but of the other two, one was built by Metro Cammell in 1948 and the fourth by Cravens in 1947. 'Hemelite' was stencilled on in yellow paint. However, when BR discovered their existence a ban was imposed on all movement on the line, even threatening to clip the points at the end of their works. In an effort to prevent this happening, the wagons were stood with their wheels on the points, although the company did accept the ban.

On Sunday 1st July, 1979 the point rodding and fittings between Harpenden Junction signal box and the branch points were removed, along with the branch shunting signal. The points from the fast lines were clipped out of use but were not removed until 21st March, 1980. The branch was finally severed on 24th July, 1979, when the first two lengths of track were lifted. The signal box finally closed on 20th October, 1979.

Hemelite disposed of its Drewry locomotive to the Yorkshire Dales Railway and it made its last journey to Redbourn on 7th February, 1982, from where it was collected by low-loader lorry the next morning. With the rest of the BR network closed by an ASLEF strike, this was the only movement on BR rails that day.

The Hemelite Drewry locomotive at Redbourn awaiting transportation to the Yorkshire Dales Railway at Embsay, 7th February, 1982.   *Authors*

Track lifting at 27¼ milepost, March 1982. *Authors' Collection*

The sharp curve away from Harpenden Junction, 27th April, 1982. *Authors' Collection*

Chapter Fifteen

Up With the Old, Down With the New

Early in 1980 a 'Save the Nickey Group' was formed in Harpenden, with the aim of getting the line working again, in the hope that Hemelite would return to moving ash by rail instead of road. As a way of making the proposal more attractive, from a commercial point of view, the group suggested that a refuse disposal depot planned for the area should be located at Cupid Green, which could make use of the branch.

A public meeting was held on 5th March to gain support for their ideas, prior to a County Council meeting on 13th March, at which the issue was to be discussed. The meeting was attended by more railway enthusiasts than general public, and in any case by that time British Railways had made it clear there was no future for the line. Any plans for saving the branch came far too late to change the minds of those in authority, and the line's fate was sealed by the hands and cutting torches of the demolition men.

Track-lifting proceeded from Claydale Sidings on 8th February, 1982. The iron bridge over the brickworks' access road was removed on 28th February, giving unrestricted access to the works. On 21st April, near the 25¾ milepost, the contractors' cutting gear set fire to the dry undergrowth on the bank, necessitating a visit from the fire brigade.

All the scrap metal had been removed by lorry, the final load being lifted by the site of Harpenden Junction signal box on 27th April. As the lorry turned to leave, its rear wheels fell through the cover of the signal box cesspit, and heavy lifting gear had to be called in. Another contractor followed to collect up the sleepers, but many rotten ones were burnt on site.

On 18th June, 1982 it was announced that the brick arch bridge over Luton Road at Harpenden was to be removed and accordingly in October a notice of road closure was advertised. However, at the last moment, this notice was withdrawn because it was realised that if the planned public path became a reality, then the bridge would be needed to afford a safe crossing of the main road.

The public path proposal went ahead and plans were passed in August 1983, which involved creating a walkway from Harpenden right through to Hemel Hempstead, using the route of the railway. Clearance work started the following month. However, the path was to be bisected by the Redbourn By-Pass, the coming of which finally saw the end of the problem bridges over Harpenden Lane and Chequers Lane.

Path laying started in November 1983 at Harpenden and two years later steps were provided at Ambrose Lane and Luton Road bridges to give access. On Sunday 1st December, 1985 the Mayor of St Albans declared the path open and planted a tree on the site of Redbourn station. A number of new footpath notices, bearing the name of the 'Nicky Way', were erected. The design for these came from a competition.

At Roundwood Halt, part of the platform had survived the demolition process and the concrete signal post, which also escaped, underwent a refit

Tracklifting at Roundwood Halt, 21st May, 1982. *Authors' Collection*

Three Cherry Trees Lane, with the trackbed in use as a footpath, March 1993.*Authors' Collection*

(carried out by one of the authors) in July 1984. This still serves as a reminder to path-users of the route's railway history. Although reasonably well used by the public and schoolchildren, very little maintenance was carried out, and many trees and bushes encroached upon the walkway.

Efforts had been made for a long time to complete the route through to Hemel Hempstead, and in February 1990 access was provided at Three Cherry Trees Lane, Hemel Hempstead, and the bridge there was repainted. Eventually the missing bridge deck at the entrance to Hemelite's works at Cupid Green was replaced and this made it possible to trace the complete route back to the bridge by the former Midland station in Hemel Hempstead.

Representatives from local Councils and the Countryside Commission met at Midland Road bridge on Sunday 24th January, 1993 to re-open officially the whole path, as a footpath and cycleway. The Mayor of Dacorum, John Buteux, cut the ribbon, and a pamphlet was produced to promote the route. Guests then returned to the Old Town Hall at Hemel Hempstead for refreshments, just as they did when the railway opened. New white-on-green signs were erected along the route of the path in December 1993.

Although safety railings had been installed on either side of the pathway on top of Luton Road bridge at Harpenden, soon after its opening in 1985, these were considered (in 1995) to be an insufficient safety measure. There was also a problem with tree roots which were penetrating the bridge brickwork and so work was carried out to remove all the trees, together with the earth embankment over the bridge. The path was then relaid at its lower level, new railings were erected and spikes fitted on the parapets to stop children from walking along the edge and sitting over the main road. Some repointing was carried out at the same time. However, at the time of writing, the brickwork under the arch appears very wet and some parts of the bridge are affected by large cracks - in other words, we are back where we started at the time of Yolland's report of 1876!

Woodend Lane looking towards Hemel Hempstead showing the footpath on the trackbed, March 1993.   *Authors' Collection*

Chapter Sixteen

Questions - But Few Answers

Why the 'Nickey Line'?

In common with most other small railway lines, this one acquired a nickname. At Hemel Hempstead people referred to 'Puffing Annie' or 'Gentle Annie', which related to the rolling stock rather than the line itself. However, at the Harpenden end it was, and still is, referred to as the 'Nickey Line'.

The *Harpenden Free Press*, soon after World War II, discussed the origins of this title (which proves the name is not a recent invention). Edwin Grey, who was noted for his local knowledge, and whose friend, Wilf Roberts, helped to build the Luton Road bridge (known locally as The Arch), believed that a nickname had been used since before the railway opened. He believed it was called the 'Knickerbocker Railway' which, over the years, has been shortened to the 'Nickey Line'.

Various suggestions have been put forward as to the origin of this name. One seems to point to the navvies who built the line wearing knickerbockers, whilst another relates to the short trousers worn by the many schoolboys who used the line. Another variation on this theme says that the line was a 'shortened version' of that originally planned, but older residents of the area say it relates to the sound of the engine exhaust as it climbed up the incline to Roundwood, puffing 'knickerbocker, knickerbocker'. Then there is the engine drivers' expression 'Down the nick', meaning to run out of steam, which was very relevant to this stretch of line, as engines sometimes had to make more than one attempt to get up the Roundwood incline.

Other theories include reference to the parish of St Nicholas, a funicular line, the line being opened 'in the nick of time' or even that it was 'as slow as old Nick'. If, indeed, the name came before the line opened, then some of these theories can be discounted, but at present it is fair to say that no-one knows for sure just how, or why, the 'Nickey Line' got its name.

When the *Harpenden Free Press* wrote about the line it spelled 'Nickey' with an 'e', and in fact when special trains were run in latter days, their headboards and tickets appeared with the 'e' included. It is strange, therefore, that official signs have recently been erected directing the public to the 'Nicky Line Footpath and Cycle Way'.

'The Local Worthy . . .'

Some years ago a magazine stated 'the local worthy responsible for the Harpenden to Hemel Hempstead Railway died penniless in the workhouse', but it mentioned no name.

Whilst the financial dealings of the concern may lead one to put some credence in this story, our researches have shown that none of the principal players in this drama ever descended to such miserable depths. In fact, John Grover, who did have local connections, and whose idea started it all, died at his home on Clapham Common in August 1892, after a lingering illness, and is buried nearby. He was a well-known, well-respected member of his community and most certainly did not die a pauper. As we know, John Barrow died a wealthy man, and his son, John James, also (but these were not local men).

Mr Stallon was the only other prominent local figure at the outset, but he had little to do with the railway during building - save to guard Hemel Hempstead's interests from his vantage point on many public committees. In life he was very outspoken, and not always popular (the editorial announcing his death commenced with 'And so Mr Samuel Stallon has passed away at last'!). His obituary did concede, though, that, had he died in Hemel Hempstead, he would have had an imposing funeral and that what he did not know about public life was not worth knowing. In fact, he died in Bournemouth on 11th May, 1906, aged 84 years. This man was certainly not the workhouse inmate we needed to find.

The conclusion is, therefore, that the workhouse story is a complete myth.

Footnote!

It is also fair to say that this book would not have been completed but for the accident suffered by co-author, Geoff, when he broke his leg whilst walking on the 'Nickey' path! The enforced 'rest' made it all possible. We hope you enjoy the end-product.

Appendix One

Bridge Numbers Applicable to the Branch

1	Ambrose Lane, Harpenden
2	A6 (now A1081) Luton Road, Harpenden
2B	Roundwood Footbridge
2A	Culvert
3	B487 - Harpenden Lane, Redbourn
4	A5 (A5183) - Redbourn
5	River Ver
6	Chequers Lane, Redbourn
6A	Culvert
6B	Culvert
6D	M1 Motorway
6C	Water Pipe
7	Wood End Lane
8	Three Cherry Trees Lane, Cupid Green
9	Claydale Brickworks
10	High Street Green, Hemel Hempstead
11	Footbridge, Godwin's Halt
12	Footbridge, Highfield
13	Footbridge, Highfield
14	Highfield Lane (now Queensway), Hemel Hempstead
14A	Culvert
15	Junction of Adeyfield Road, St Albans Road and Midland Road
16	Infirmary Lane/Hillfield Road
17	Albion Hill, Paradise
18	Marlowes Viaduct
19	Footpath, Moor End
19A	Culvert, Heath Park
20	Station Road
21	Corner Hall Road
22	Grand Junction (Union) Canal
23	Cattle Creep, Boxmoor
24	River Bulbourne
25	A41 - London Road, Boxmoor
26	Roughdown Road

Queensway bridge, Hemel Hempstead, August 1960.   *K. Taylor*

156

Appendix Two

Thoughts at Roundwood

1. Nobody knows where the thing goes,
    Two trains on a single track per day,
    One in the morning, one in the evening,
    Nothing to go for or go to they say.

2. Block and tackle, pulley and crane,
    Strained and groaned for many a day
    Flinging a sturdy span for ever
    Over two trains that pass this way.

3. Two or two hundred! The rules insist
    Upon a competent official
    To start at dawn and stop at dusk,
    His industry with flag and whistle.

4. One in the morning, one in the evening,
    Thudding through in a smoking smother,
    Only a breathing space between
    To get ready for another.

5. Thinking of hundreds already spent
    To raise a steel path in the sky,
    Fifty quid after all is a mere flea bite
    For letting two trains go by.

An anonymous offering to the local press in 1952, following the rebuilding of Roundwood footbridge. Harpenden UDC received a bill for £51 from BR, for the services of a flagman to warn of the two trains each day which used the branch.

A 1943 view of Roundwood Halt showing the old footbridge. *Ken Allen*

The Closing of Harpenden Junction Signal Box

1.   The signal went up and the train passed by,
The signal went down, and you heaved a sigh
As you entered in the train and the time
And added 'Box Closed' on the very next line.

2.   You looked around, and your heart beat fast,
As your mind recalled the days gone past;
Through daytime and night-time, winter and spring,
You've heaved on the levers and heard the bells ring.

3.   You've polished the lino, until it shone -
Hang up your duster, those days have gone.
Take home the Brasso - the plates need not shine,
For them and for you, its the end of the line.

4.   The fire in the stove will soon burn itself out
And the clock will stop ticking without a doubt,
For there's no-one to stoke and no-one to wind -
When 'progress' takes over, you're left behind.

5.   So they made you redundant, loyal servant, good friend,
Your railway duties are now at an end,
So put on your coat, turn the key in the door,
Then hang up your uniform - you'll need it no more!

Sue Woodward

The interior of Harpenden Junction signal box. Note the signalling diagram clearly showing the Hemel Hempstead branch, 21st March, 1978. *A. Turner*

Ode to the Arch

1. Oh Nickey Bridge!
    How often have I passed within your shadow
    Or, as a child, raised my voice
    And listened for the echo?
    How many times you offered me
    A shelter from the rain,
    Or I rushed to stand beneath your arch
    To hear the rumble of a train.

2. Oh Nickey Bridge!
    When you were built you spanned a dusty turnpike way
    And bore a steam train on your back -
    Alas, it is not so today!
    'Tis tarmacadamed road and paving stones
    Which lie beneath your graceful curve,
    Upon which juggernauts and other kinds of traffic
    Do haste, and hoot, and swerve.

3. Oh Nickey Bridge!
    The trains you used to carry have now all passed away,
    Your iron road has been removed
    And now you, too, are doomed, they say!
    I know your tiny pavement is a hazard
    And your brickwork cracks apart
    But, to me, 'The Arch' is a landmark
    With a special place in my heart.

4. So Nickey Bridge -
    If doomed you are - farewell to you, old friend,
    But here I put on record
    I loved you to the end!

Poem written when it was announced that the Luton Road bridge was to be demolished.
As it turned out, it was reprieved, and still stands.

Sue Woodward

Acknowledgements

We are grateful to the following for their help and encouragement during the writing of this book:

Ken Allen

Les Casey

Eric Edwards

Rodney Flanagan

Geoff Goslin

Christopher Jobling

Ralph Lacy

Pauline Siddell

Michael Stanyon

Arthur Turner

Alan Wilmott

Eric Brandreth

Chris Dean

Tony Edwards

The Grover Family

John Hinson

June Kavanagh

Rodney Marshall

Smeathmans, Solicitors

Joan Thurston

Geoff Whinnett

John Wood

and the following official bodies

Boxmoor Trust

British Newspaper Library

BR - Collectors' Corner

County Record Office, Hertford

Dacorum Council

Hemel Hempstead Library

Home Counties Newspapers

House of Lords, Record Office

Luton Library

Public Record Office, Kew

and many others, too numerous to mention.

The gradient post at Roundwood Summit, showing the steepest gradient on the line, 21st April, 1956. *S. Summerson*